The
Church
Empowered

The Church Empowered

The Nature and Workings of the Holy Spirit

Frank Bateman Stanger

FRANCIS ASBURY PRESS
of Zondervan Publishing House
Grand Rapids, Michigan

Francis Asbury Press is an imprint of Zondervan Publishing House,
1415 Lake Drive, S.E., Grand Rapids, Michigan 49506.

Library of Congress Cataloging in Publication Data

Stanger, Frank Bateman.
    The church empowered : the nature and workings of the Holy Spirit
/ Frank Bateman Stanger.
        p.   cm.
    ISBN 0-310-75461-5
    1. Holy Spirit. 2. Church. I. Title.
BT121.2.S79   1989
231'.3–dc20   89-37621
                                                                        CIP

Edited by Lois Kempton

Printed in the United States of America

89   90   91   92   93   94   95 / ML / 10   9   8   7   6   5   4   3   2   1

CONTENTS

Frank Bateman Stanger died before he was able to finish the citations. His former secretary, Mrs. Harriett Jenkins, of Lexington, Kentucky, and Mrs. Eunice Weldon, research librarian at the B. L. Fisher Library at Asbury Theological Seminary, have been of immeasureable assistance. However, some notes are incomplete and a number of quotations have been impossible to trace.

FOREWORD

A mighty volume of words is being written and spoken these days about the Holy Spirit. What an amazing contrast to the days when I began my ministry in The Methodist Church! Two incidents come to mind. On one occasion I overheard a distinguished minister say to an effective evangelist that he should give less attention to the Holy Spirit in his preaching and more to Jesus Christ. And I will never forget the day when I, as a young minister, was warned by a person that I should beware of preaching too much about the Holy Spirit, lest my future ministry be destroyed.

How times have changed! Now if you don't preach at least every other sermon on the Holy Spirit, in some circles you are considered unspiritual. Holy Spirit conferences and seminars are held everywhere. Series after series of sermons on the Holy Spirit are preached. To some it seems almost like supersaturation. I heard of a friend who was asked to go hear a certain well-known speaker who would be giving a week-long series on the Holy Spirit. My friend's immediate response was: "Not that again!" (But the story had a happy ending. My friend heard the speaker, and was greatly blessed.)

Why another book on the Holy Spirit? The best I can do is to share my motivation in writing. From the time I became a Christian I have been deeply interested in the person and work of the Holy Spirit. I have spent my entire vocational life fulfilling assignments prescribed by Wesleyan parameters. These have added constant fuel to a fire in whose warmth I have rejoiced and whose sparks, I trust, have been scattered everywhere I have ministered.

The contents of this book represent the results of my life-long study and experience of the Holy Spirit. Every conviction that is expressed has already been proved in the crucible of my own life. The pages that follow are not intended to conform rigidly to any pre-determined theological mold, but they honestly and confidently express my "head-felt" and heart-felt belief in the Third Person of the Trinity.

My background has been both pastoral and academic. In all my preaching about the Holy Spirit, I sought to be intellectually credible in the light of the revelations of Holy Scripture. Just so, in all my teaching I could not escape the pastoral insistence that, to be relevant, truth about the Holy Spirit must be functional in human experience, not merely theoretical.

My desire as I write can be stated thus: (1) that each Christian will experience the baptism of the Holy Spirit; (2) that each Spirit-filled Christian will share in the personal ministries of the Holy Spirit; and (3) that Spirit-filled Christians will be instrumental in relating the power of the Holy Spirit to their local churches.

May every reader be willing to pray:

> Holy Spirit, truth divine
>   Dawn upon this soul of mine;
> Word of God and inward light,
>   Wake my Spirit, clear my sight.
>   Samuel Longfellow

1 | IS THE HOLY SPIRIT A LUXURY OR A NECESSITY?

> Which of you fathers, if your son asks for a fish, will give him a snake instead? Or if he asks for an egg, will give him a scorpion? If you then, though you are evil, know how to give good gifts to your children, how much more will your Father in heaven give the Holy Spirit to those who ask him!
>
> *(Luke 11:11–13)*

There is a radical difference between a luxury and a necessity. A luxury is an expensive rarity—something that may be pleasing to possess, but which is not necessary for living. On the other hand, a necessity is essential to life. Without such a necessity life either deteriorates or perishes.

I remember the first time I ever saw more than one radio in a home. In my first full-time pastorate, one home I visited had a small radio on the kitchen counter, a large console radio in the living room, and a medium-size radio in a bedroom upstairs. In contrast to the necessities of life, three radios are a luxury.

I heard of a couple who had three homes: a winter home in Florida, a summer home in Maine, and a home on the Main Line in Philadelphia where they stopped off between trips. One home is a necessity. But what about three?

One minister visited a family in his parish where he noticed there were five automobiles parked out front. Discovering that there were only four members of the family, he dared to ask about the extra car. "Oh," said the

11

father, "each of us owns a car, but we keep a spare car parked along the curb in the event that any of our cars are hemmed in by one of the others." Luxury or necessity? You be the judge.

Speaking spiritually, down across the centuries there have been but two basic attitudes toward the Holy Spirit: He has been considered either a mere luxury or a necessity.

Some have assumed that a relationship to the Holy Spirit is only a luxury. They admit that the Holy Spirit is needed by certain individuals whom God has called for particular assignments, but not by ordinary rank and file believers. Such a concept belongs to the Old Testament dispensation.

Others assume that it takes a certain mystical type of temperament to receive the Holy Spirit, a temperament which most people do not possess. I shall always remember a charming, cultured lady in one of my early churches. She was faithful at the morning worship services and contributed at least moderately to the budget of the church. She always seemed appreciative of my preaching, and often expressed commendation. On my last Sunday at that church, she bade me farewell, remarking, "Thank you for your sermons, but you have talked about things I am not capable of experiencing."

There are yet others who believe that you can count on the power of the Holy Spirit only in times of special crisis. And some folks say that a Christian must choose between the practical and the mystical in religion. They think of the people who focus upon the Holy Spirit and personal spirituality as mystical but not practical. They want a religion which is less "heavenly minded" and more "earthly good."

All of these who consider the Holy Spirit only a luxury are settling for a more nominal type of religious profession and are deficient in spiritual power. Many are ignorant about the Holy Spirit and can be taught. Others may be stubborn and resistant and must be prayed for. Nevertheless, living by the "luxury view" is evidence of sub-normal Christian experience and contrary to what God intended.

Is the Holy Spirit a luxury or a necessity? Let us listen to six mighty voices that eloquently proclaim His necessity.

THE ANSWER OF THE OLD TESTAMENT

The Old Testament Scriptures conclusively reveal the indispensability of the activity of the Holy Spirit in the sovereign plans of God for the world. The Holy Spirit is not an original discovery of the twentieth century. In the light of the Scriptures, He is to be viewed in His eternal personhood.

Various names are given to the Holy Spirit in the Old Testament, such as the Spirit, my Spirit, the Spirit of God, the Spirit of Jehovah, the Spirit of the Living God, The Spirit of the Lord, the Spirit of Burning, the Spirit of Holiness.

Likewise, there are various symbols of the Holy Spirit in the Bible:

Dove: (Gen. 8:8–12; Song 5:2; 6:9, Matt. 3:16, 10:16; John 16:13)

Water: (Num. 20:11; Isa. 41:18; John 4:14; 7:37 39; 1 Cor. 10:4; Rev. 21:6)

Fire: (Ex. 3:2–6; Isa. 4:4; Matt. 3:11; Acts 2:3)

Wind: (Gen. 2:7; Isa. 30:28; Ezek. 37:9; John 3:3–8; 20:22; Acts 2:2)

(The Hebrew word for *spirit* is *rûach* meaning wind, breath, mind, consciousness; it is used 400 times in the Old Testament.)

Wine: (Ps. 104:15; Acts 2:13; Eph. 5:18)

Oil: (Ex. 30:23–33; Isa. 61:1; Acts 10:38; 2 Cor. 1:21)

The Holy Spirit was active in the original creation. "Now the earth was formless and empty, darkness was over the surface of the deep, and the Spirit of God was hovering over the waters" (Gen. 1:2). "Then God said, 'Let us make man in our image, in our likeness' "(Gen. 1:26). "The LORD God formed the man from the dust of the ground and breathed into his nostrils the breath ['ruach'] of life, and man became a living being" (Gen. 2:7). Just so, the Holy Spirit is the source of all created life. "The Spirit of God has made me; the breath of the Almighty gives me life" (Job 33:4).

From the beginning the Holy Spirit has been active continuously in the providential preservation of life. "In his hand is the life of every creature and the breath of all mankind" (Job 12:10). "When you take away their breath, they die and return to the dust" (Ps. 104:29). A New Testament writer said centuries later, "In him we live and move and have our being" (Acts 17:28).

The Holy Spirit was active in the Old Testament theocracy, which was the form of government under which God's people lived. God ruled His people through divinely selected leaders. So we find the Holy Spirit active in the selection, anointing, and empowerment of leaders. "The Spirit of God came upon [Saul] in power" (1 Sam. 11:6). "Samuel took the horn of oil and anointed [David] in the presence of his brothers; and from that day on the Spirit of the LORD came upon David in power" (1 Sam. 16:13). We discover the same process of empowerment after the divine selection of each of the judges—"The Spirit of the LORD came upon him" (Judg. 3:10; 6:34; 11:29; 14:6, 19; 15:14).

Within the theocracy the Holy Spirit was the source of the prophets' inspiration. They were the conscience of the nation in regard to personal sins and social evils. The call of every prophet was attributed to the Spirit of God, and particular utterances and activities of the prophets were under the inspiration of the Divine Spirit. Take, for illustration, the prophet Amos. Note such descriptive references as these to the divine leadership through the inspiration of the Spirit: "The LORD took me from tending the flock and said to me, 'Go prophesy to my people Israel'" (Amos 7:15). "Hear this word the LORD has spoken against you" (3:1). "The Sovereign LORD showed me" (7:1).

The Holy Spirit bestowed special abilities upon individuals selected for divinely appointed work. Exodus 31:1–11 tells about the Lord giving "ability and knowledge" to and filling with His Spirit those who were to devise artistic designs; work in gold, silver, and bronze; cut stones; carve wood; fashion the furnishings of the tabernacle and the ark of the covenant; and even make the garments of the priests with their delicate and detailed embroidery.

The Old Testament Scriptures also reveal the power of the Spirit as He restrained and resisted those who were the enemies of the theocracy. Foreign armies were destroyed, and opposing leaders were rendered ineffective. The Spirit was God's minister, both in the establishment and continuity of the theocracy.

The activity of the Holy Spirit during the Old Testament dispensation is seen also in the manner in which the meaning of faith was illumined for the forerunner of a new dispensation that was to be characterized by "righteousness through faith."

Abraham believed God and it was counted to him for righteousness (Gen. 15:6; Rom. 4:3). The psalmist declares that Phinehas, the grandson of Aaron, secured the cessation of the plague that was destroying the nation (Num. 25:7–11), and "this was credited to him as righteousness for endless generations to come" (Ps. 106:30–31).

In the New Testament the writer of the epistle to the Hebrews declares that Old Testament personages Abel, Enoch, Noah, Abraham, Sarah, Isaac, Jacob, Joseph, Moses, Rahab, Gideon, Barak, Samson, Jephthah, David, Samuel, and the prophets had valid insights into the meaning of faith. These were inspired and developed by the Holy Spirit.

The Old Testament prophets served not merely as the conscience of the theocracy, but as the proclaimers and preservers of divine revelations concerning the coming Messiah. Who can read the awe-inspiring words of Isaiah 52:13–53:12 about the coming Messiah, and not be convinced of a higher inspiration?

The Holy Spirit was active in the call, inspiration, and utterances of the prophets, both oral and written; and in the preservation and collection of the oral traditions into the Old Testament canon of Holy Scripture.

The Apostle Peter summarizes it well, " . . . no prophecy of Scripture came about by the prophet's own interpretation. For prophecy never had its origin in the will of man, but men spoke from God as they were carried along by the Holy Spirit" (2 Peter 1:20–21).

Finally, the Holy Spirit pointed those in the old dispensation to the New Covenant, the New Creation. Ezekiel 36:25–27 is a key passage: "I will sprinkle clean water on you, and you will be clean; I will cleanse you from all your impurities and from all your idols. I will give you a new heart and put a new spirit within you; I will remove from you your heart of stone and give you a heart of flesh. And I will put my Spirit in you and move you to follow in my decrees and be careful to keep my laws."

In summary, in the Old Testament the Holy Spirit was given to special individuals to fit them for particular services; in the New Testament the Spirit is poured out on all flesh. In the Old Testament the Holy Spirit was *with* persons and *upon* them; in the New Testament the Spirit dwells *in persons*. In the Old Testament the Holy Spirit took the initiative in coming to a selected person, for a special purpose, and His empowering presence was sometimes transitory. In the New Testament a covenant relationship exists between the Holy Spirit and the consecrated person, a permanent abiding of the Holy Spirit within the believer.

Under the Old Testament dispensation the Holy Spirit was not resident upon the earth, but visited it from time to time as occasion required. However, in the New Dispensation the Spirit of God is dwelling upon the earth.

In the Old Testament the Holy Spirit came as the Spirit of the Father; in the New Testament He comes as the Spirit of the Son. Thus, most Christians across the centuries have affirmed the Holy Spirit as "proceeding from both the Father and the Son."

THE ANSWER OF JESUS CHRIST

Is the Holy Spirit a luxury or a necessity? We turn now to the New Testament and the answer of Jesus Christ.

The Gospels impressively demonstrate the prominence of the Holy Spirit in the life and ministry of Jesus. The Holy Spirit had predicted through the prophets the coming of the

Messiah (1 Peter 1:11). Such predictions included the fact that the Holy Spirit would be upon the Messiah (Isa. 11:2–4; 42:1–4; 61:1–4). The record of the confirmation of these predictions are found in Matthew 3:16; John 1:32; and Acts 10:38.

The Holy Spirit was the divine agent in the incarnation of God in Jesus Christ. Jesus was conceived by the Holy Spirit (Matt. 1:20; Luke 1:35) and born of the Virgin Mary (Luke 2:7). The Holy Spirit superintended the symmetrical development of Jesus. He "grew in wisdom and stature, and in favor with God and men" (Luke 2:52; cf. v. 40). The Holy Spirit initiated and sustained the messianic consciousness of the incarnate Christ (Matt. 3:17; Luke 2:49; 10:21–24; John 10:30).

The Holy Spirit was the source of Christ's personal sanctification. John writes that the Spirit possessed Christ fully (John 3:34). In His high-priestly prayer at the close of His earthly ministry, Christ declared that He had sanctified Himself in order that His disciples might also be sanctified through the truth (John 17:19).

The Holy Spirit was the inspiration of Christ's personal mystical experiences. Such experiences of the divine, of the spiritual world, are "numinous," that is, received apart from any intermediary agents. Such mystical experiences in the life of Jesus are illustrated by His vision of seeing Satan fall from heaven as lightning (Luke 10:18) and the appearance with Him of Moses and Elijah at the Transfiguration (Matt. 17:2; Mark 9:2; Luke 9:29).

The entire ministry of Jesus was made possible by the Holy Spirit. At His baptism the Spirit descended upon Him like a dove (Matt. 3:16). In the wilderness temptation He resisted Satan through the power of the Spirit (Luke 4:1). Jesus' inaugural sermon in the synagogue in His hometown of Nazareth was His acknowledgment of the anointing of the Holy Spirit upon Him. "The Spirit of the Lord is upon me, because he has anointed me to preach . . . to proclaim . . . to release" (Luke 4:16–21).

All of Jesus' teachings were under the inspiration of the Holy Spirit. He spoke with divine authority, not as the scribes spoke (Matt. 7:29; Mark 1:22). Jesus' ministry of healing and doing good was in the power of the Spirit (Matt. 12:28; Luke 4:18; Acts 10:38). In all of these works Jesus was recognized by Satan (the "unholy spirit") as possessing the Holy Spirit (Mark 1:24).

The Holy Spirit made possible the atoning benefits of Christ's death upon the cross. The writer of the epistle to the Hebrews says, "Christ . . . through the eternal Spirit offered himself unblemished to God" (9:14). The Holy Spirit also applies to individuals the benefits of such redemption.

Jesus Christ was raised from the dead by the power of the Holy Spirit (Rom. 1:4; 8:11). The Spirit was also the active agent in His post-resurrection ministry (Acts 1:2). The resurrected Christ ascended to heaven in the power of the Spirit (Acts 1:9). Christ's present ministry of intercession at the right hand of God is related both to the Spirit in the heavenlies and to the Spirit's application of His intercessions in our lives (Rom. 8:24, 26–27).

Jesus Christ will return to earth in the power of the Holy Spirit. It is the Spirit who keeps alive, within the Christian community, the hope of Christ's second advent. "The Spirit and the bride say, 'Come!'" (Rev. 22:17) "He who testifies to these things says, 'Yes, I am coming soon.' Amen. Come, Lord Jesus!" (Rev. 22:20).

In addition to His life and ministry the teachings of Jesus also confirm the indispensability of the Holy Spirit. Recall Luke 11:13. Jesus was talking about earthly parents giving necessary things to their children. Bread, eggs, and fish are necessities, not luxuries. Then He draws the analogy: "If you then, though you are evil, know how to give good gifts to your children, how much more will your Father in heaven give the Holy Spirit to those who ask him!"

Some general observations may be noted about Jesus' teachings concerning the Holy Spirit. First, He reserved most of them for the closing days of His ministry. Certainly this reveals their importance.

Second, practically all of His teachings were communicated to the disciples in particular, not to everyone in general. He saw that it was impossible for "the world" to see or know or receive the Spirit (John 14:17). So we deduce that the experience of the fullness of the Holy Spirit, the norm pictured in the New Testament Scriptures, is related to those who already profess their faith in Christ and not to the unregenerate.

Third, Jesus always spoke of the Holy Spirit as an experience, not a doctrine. He never spoke of merely believing in the Holy Spirit, but of receiving Him.

Fourth, the coming of the Holy Spirit is always spoken of as a gift, the fulfillment of a divine promise (Luke 11:13; John 20:22; Acts 1:4).

Finally, Jesus always spoke of the ministry of the Holy Spirit in its vital relationship to Himself. "The Father will give you another Counselor" (John 14:16). Who was the first Counselor? Jesus, of course. The ministry of the Holy Spirit is never to glorify Himself, but always to glorify Christ (John 16:13–15). The Spirit always testifies to Christ (John 14:26): who He is, His words, what He has done and suffered, what He is to achieve. Martin Luther wrote, "We could never come to know the Father's grace without Christ, so we would know nothing of Christ save through the revelation of the Holy Spirit."

Generally speaking, the teachings of Jesus concerning the Holy Spirit may be grouped under three headings.

First, Jesus taught that the Holy Spirit is the source of *life*. He provides its beginning through the new birth (John 3:5). He provides satisfaction of life, through the "streams of living water" flowing through the Spirit-filled person (John 7:37–39). And the Spirit provides the hope of everlasting life in the immediate presence of God (John 14:16).

Second, Jesus taught that the Holy Spirit is the source of *illumination*. Jesus speaks of Him as a personal teacher (John 14:26). He is the revealer of truth (John 14:17). The world is a realm of deceits and illusions by which the mind of even the Christian disciple, left to itself, might easily be led astray; but in the Spirit of truth the disciple has a safeguard against the world's subtleties and sophistications.

The Holy Spirit makes manifest the fullness of truth as it is in Jesus Christ. He reminds the Christian of the Master's

teachings (John 14:26). When events and facts are repro-
duced by the Spirit, they are not like the sometimes
misleading revelations of an amateur photographer, but like
the work of a great painter. The Spirit's reminders capture
the essence of truth better than the most literal recollections
would be.

The Holy Spirit applies the teachings of Christ to all
relationships of life (John 16:13). Jesus is greater than His
words. When He left the world many things remained
unuttered. But the Spirit takes His words and opens up their
full meaning in all their dimensions. He relates Christ and
His words to all our dealings with others.

We have heard often "Christ is the answer." Perhaps it
is truer to say that Christ is the way to the answer rather
than being the answer in a neat, predetermined, handed-
down capsule of truth. Jesus does not always take away our
problems, but He gives us a new base from which to deal
with them. He throws light on every situation in which He
is invited to be present.

The Holy Spirit illuminates our utterance in the time of
need. "You will be given what to say, for it will not be you
speaking, but the Spirit of your Father speaking through
you" (Matt. 10:19–20). "[They] began to speak . . . as the
Spirit enabled them" (Acts 2:4). Concerning the Holy Spirit
as the source of illumination, we can appreciate Oswald
Chambers' prayer: "O Lord, cause my intellect to glow with
thy Holy Spirit's teaching."

Even more than these, Jesus taught that the Holy Spirit
is also the source of *power*. This was Christ's promise to His
disciples just before He ascended into heaven: "You will
receive power when the Holy Spirit comes on you" (Acts
1:8). The reception of the Spirit is the possession of Christ in
the fullness of His redeeming power. The Spirit was sent on
the ground of Christ's death, resurrection, and exaltation.
Thus the disciples did not lose Christ. Rather, they now
possessed Him in the power in which He lives and reigns
(John 16:7).

Power is adequacy: the ability to become and to do
what God intends and Christ assigns. The Holy Spirit is the

source of power for daily living. The Holy Spirit is an "advocate," a "counselor"—"another Comforter." Formerly, the disciples had received their strength directly from Christ. Now they get their strength from the Holy Spirit who has taken the place of Christ.

The Holy Spirit is the source of power for effective witnessing to Jesus Christ. According to Jesus this is the prime objective of the Christian's being filled with the power of the Spirit ("you will be my witnesses" [Acts 1:8]). The Holy Spirit is power for effective evangelism in the world. "I will send him to you. When he comes, he will convict the world of guilt in regard to sin and righteousness and judgment" (John 16:7–8). It is the Spirit's function to convict the world, to reach its conscience, to illumine righteousness in contrast to sin. This conviction is accomplished through the ministry of the Christians through whom the Spirit works.

The spiritual possibilities of the Christian seem to be unlimited in light of the power of the Holy Spirit. Recall the words of Jesus: "Anyone who has faith in me will do what I have been doing. He will do even greater things than these, because I am going to the Father" (John 14:12).

Jesus always spoke of the Holy Spirit as God's gift through Him to His disciples. "I will ask the Father, and he will give you another Counselor to be with you forever— the Spirit of truth" (John 14:16–17). "The Counselor, the Holy Spirit, whom the Father will send in my name" (John 14:26). "I will send him to you" (John 16:7). In the Upper Room, after the Resurrection, Jesus breathed on His disciples, and said to them, "Receive the Holy Spirit" (John 20:22).

Note that Jesus spoke in the imperative mood to His disciples about receiving the Holy Spirit. " . . . but stay in the city, until you have been clothed with power from on high" (Luke 24:49). The Acts of the Apostles opens with the resurrected Lord charging His disciples, "Do not leave Jerusalem, but wait for the gift my Father promised" (Acts 1:4). Inherent in such a command is Jesus' concept of the necessity of the Holy Spirit in both spiritual experience and

Christian ministry. Jesus never wasted words on trivial matters. To Him the experience of the Holy Spirit was the basic importance.

THE ANSWER OF THE EARLY CHURCH

We turn now to the early church. The book of Acts is the historical record of the earliest period in the life of the Christian church, and the New Testament epistles reveal the earliest Christian theological emphases and ethical practices. These affirm the validity of the person and ministry of the Holy Spirit.

The opening chapters of Acts tell the story of the descent of the Holy Spirit on the Day of Pentecost. This is the key to everything else that is recorded in the entire book. One cannot imagine the early church without Pentecost.

The Holy Spirit provided power, adequacy, and ability along numerous avenues, both to individuals and to the corporate church:

Power to be united with one another in love (Acts 2:42, 46; 4:32)

Power to reveal Jesus Christ in personal living (Acts 4:13)

Power to interpret the Scriptures (Acts 2:16, 25)

Power to give persuasive witness to Christ (Acts 1:8; 2:37)

Power to perform mighty works (Acts 5:12)

Power to remain humble (Acts 3:12, 16; 14:11–18)

Power to heal (Acts 5:15)

Power to provide for material needs (Acts 2:45)

Power to be courageous in the midst of opposition (Acts 4:31)

Power to be uncompromising in conviction (Acts 5:29)

Power to be masters, never mastered—to be victors, never victims (Acts 8:4; 16:25)

Power to remain joyful, in spite of persecution (Acts 5:41)

Power to forgive (Acts 7:59–60)

Power to be divinely guided (Acts 13:2; 16:10)

Power to increase in zeal (Acts 5:42) (This is working against the natural grain—the human tendency is burn-out.)

Power to adjust to current situations (Acts 6:1–4)

Power to respond to radical revelations as ethical and social situations demand (Acts 10:28–29, 34)

Power to be spiritually creative (Acts 2:17; 13:2–3)

Power for the church to grow (Acts 2:47)

Power to persevere (Acts 26:19; 2 Tim. 4:7)

THE ANSWER OF THE CHRISTIAN CENTURIES

The clear witness of the Christian centuries to the person and work of the Holy Spirit must also be considered. Such a witness is at least twofold: the testimony of the church as a divine institution, and the testimony of individuals within the church.

Henry Van Dusen, in his book *Spirit, Son and Father,* states that the pilgrimage of the church's idea of the Holy Spirit through the Christian centuries may be thought of in four episodes. The first period, extending from the day of Pentecost to about 400 A.D., culminated in the adoption of the official creedal interpretation of the Holy Spirit. At the Council of Nicea in 325 A.D. when Christ was declared to be fully divine ("of the same substance with the Father"), the deity of the Holy Spirit was assumed and accepted by implication, without dispute and almost without consideration.

Later, at the council in Constantinople in 381 A.D. it was affirmed that the Holy Spirit is "the Lord, the life-giver, which proceedeth from the Father [or from the Father and the Son, as Western Christendom later affirmed], which with the Father and the Son is worshiped and glorified, which spoke through the prophets."

At about 400 A.D. we pass to the second main period which continues to the Protestant Reformation. During this time the church concerned itself with the relations of the Holy Spirit, not to realities within the Godhead, but to the very mundane reality of the Christian church. The outcome was that Scripture was recognized as the official repository of the Holy Spirit's utterances; thereby, the written record was invested with divine authority, and the divine inspiration was confined within records from the past. It was asserted that the authoritative interpretation of the Scriptures was limited to councils and ecclesiastical leaders alone. Thus the Holy Spirit became, in a manner, the bondsman of the church—the same church which claims its origin in the Spirit's creative action.

The third period is that known as classic Protestantism. During the Reformation authentic freedom was reclaimed for the Holy Spirit, and the Reformers laid hold of the principle of the Spirit's inward operation upon the souls of believers. Both Martin Luther and John Calvin attributed not only all works of grace within the human heart to the work of the Holy Spirit, but also recognized Him as the only adequate power that draws persons to accept the atoning work of Christ and to manifest living faith in Him.

During the last period, which includes our day, the Holy Spirit has been rediscovered as the One who comes afresh upon Christians to revive, to reempower, and to thrust them forth across the face of the earth to carry the Good News to every creature, for the fulfillment of the Lord's final command "to teach all nations." The epoch-making spiritual renewals and revivals of the eighteenth and nineteenth centuries were direct fruit of the recovery of a true understanding of the Holy Spirit. The "rediscovery" of the Spirit in the twentieth century is one of the spiritual phenomena of the contemporary age.

The Christian centuries, in spite of times of distrust and neglect of the Holy Spirit, affirm His reality as the living and potent agent of God for the purification and empowerment of His church. The Holy Spirit is "God-near" and "God-at-work."

Space does not allow even a listing, let alone a discussion of all the spiritual greathearts of the centuries who have witnessed to the reality and efficacy of the Holy Spirit's ministry in their experience. If we scanned the spiritual biographies of the church Fathers, the saints, the Reformers, the missionaries, bishops and priests, pastors and evangelists across the centuries, we would find them replete with such testimonies. Always the ideal of personal holiness and spiritual unction was the norm, and the Holy Spirit was known to be indispensable in the experiencing of such holiness and power.

THE WESLEYAN ANSWER

Included within the answer of the Christian centuries is the Wesleyan answer. A study of John Wesley and his contemporaries reveals clearly that the Holy Spirit was always affirmed as the Divine Agent in the various stages of the Wesleyan "Order of Salvation." But even more specifically, it was John Wesley who rediscovered the medieval ideal of sanctity and made it realizable in personal experience. He declared that God had raised up the Methodists primarily to promulgate the doctrine and experience of holiness of heart and life through the indwelling, cleansing presence of the Holy Spirit.

Volumes have been written about John Wesley and his distinctive emphasis upon sanctification (or holiness or Christian perfection), but one quotation from Wesley will have to suffice at this point. He wrote:

> Many years since I saw that without holiness no man shall see the Lord. I began following after it and

inciting all with whom I have any intercourse to do the same. Ten years after, God gave me a clearer view than I had before of the way to attain this; namely, by faith in the Son of God. And immediately I declared to all, "We are saved from all sin, we are made holy by faith." This I testified in private, in public, in print; and God confirmed it by a thousand witnesses. I have continued to declare this for about thirty years, and God has continued to confirm the word by His grace.

THE ANSWER OF CONTEMPORARY NEEDS

"No Holy Spirit, no church"—this axiom has been validated repeatedly in Christian history. When the fires of the Holy Spirit have burned brightly upon its altars, the church has manifested a vital, productive ministry. But when humanism and ecclesiasticism, at the expense of the Spirit, have dominated the life of the church, the result has been sterility.

The Holy Spirit is power for the church in crisis. In a real sense, the church, because of its nature as a spiritual organism, is always in crisis. But there are times when the crisis is more pronounced and decisive. Many believe that we are living in such a time.

Most mainline churches are losing membership. Evangelistic objectives and methods have been spread so thin that soul-saving in the New Testament sense is restricted throughout the church. Various aspects of social betterment have been substituted for a vital program of Christian missions throughout the world. Many believe that with such overemphasis upon social issues and political concerns, the church is experiencing a crisis in direction.

The answer lies in the Spirit's power. Dr. Samuel H. Moffatt of Princeton in a challenging message, "Where's the Power?"[1] said:

> I'm a Presbyterian. I have order and decency up to here. But where's the power? . . . Where's the power to propel us out of our comfortable, encapsulated churches and across the world? Our members are leaving; our

missions declining. Where's the power? . . . The power
of the Holy Spirit is a cleansing power . . . it is the
power of a great joy . . . it is also the power of a great
love . . . The power is already here. The trouble is with
us. We do not call for the power; we don't get it and
then we complain that we don't have it.

He also wrote;

Don't ask me again, "Where's the power?" It's
already here.

It's power for witness to this sick and hungry, this
oppressed and frightened, this lost world. It is power
that will witness to that world that there is a Savior, that
there is a Lord, and He is Jesus Christ, and the way to
Him is through the Spirit. You shall have power when
the Spirit comes, and you shall be my witnesses to the
ends of the earth. There's the power.

And what about the needs of individual Christians for
the inner unity and cleansing and empowerment which the
Holy Spirit provides? R. Newton Flew closes his scholarly
volume, *The Idea Of Perfection In Christian Theology,*[2] with
this penetrating question: "Is salvation possible for the
subconscious? This is the real question for the seeker after
holiness in our time."

The answer is forthcoming. Instincts cannot be eradicated nor must they be suppressed. Rather, they may be
sublimated. In the language of religion they can be converted
and dedicated. The subconscious can be cleansed, converted,
controlled, and united with the purposes of the conscious
mind by, and only by, the Holy Spirit.

E. Stanley Jones deals with the same question: Can the
subconscious be transformed? He is convinced that unless
the subconscious is converted we are not fully saved. We are
only fifty percent Christian. He declares that the Christian
answer is found in the working of the Holy Spirit within the
depths of the person already converted. He writes:

For the Holy Spirit, when we surrender to His
control all we know—the conscious—and all we don't

know—the subconscious does nothing less than move in to take over, cleanse, control, and coordinate the whole of the inner life, conscious and subconscious.[3]

What more evidence is needed? The Holy Spirit is always a necessity for the Christian, never a mere luxury. Without the Spirit of Truth our sight will not be clear; without the Spirit of Love our hearts will not glow; without the Spirit of Power, our wills will be deficient in nerve and strength; without the Spirit of Right our consciences will be left to sensual, self-centered whims. Without the Holy Spirit, the church will remain behind the closed doors of ecclesiastical comfortableness, of spiritual insensitivity to the needs of a lost world. Without the fullness of the Spirit, Christian experience will be subnormal and Christian activity through the church will fall far short of its divinely-intended goals.

2 | WHAT HAPPENED AT PENTECOST?

When the day of Pentecost came. . . .

(Acts 2:1)

T he New Testament records that the fulfillment of the divine promise of the Holy Spirit, in the full manifestation of His power, occurred on the day of Pentecost (Acts 2).

Pentecost in its scriptural setting was the second of the great Jewish national festivals, whose institution is recorded in Deuteronomy 16:9–12. In the Old Testament it is called the Feast of Weeks because it was observed seven weeks after the paschal feast of the Passover. It was called Pentecost in the New Testament because it occurred fifty days after the Sabbath following the Passover.

It was instituted originally to mark the end of the wheat harvest. It had the nature of a harvest-home celebration. The day was observed in thanksgiving to God and reached its climax in the presentation of the first fruits of the harvest—two loaves of bread—unto the Lord.

WHY WAS THE HOLY SPIRIT GIVEN ON PENTECOST?

Why did God chose the day of Pentecost for the fulfillment of the promise of the coming of the Holy Spirit in His fullness (Joel 2:28–32)? For one thing, it was a national religious festival. Jews had gathered in Jerusalem from all over the world. Estimates of the number of pilgrims in Jerusalem on this occasion range from one-and-a-half million to three million. Why should not the fulfillment of the Great Commission begin auspiciously?

Pentecost was also a day of thanksgiving for a successful harvest. Could this be spiritually symbolic of the "harvest of redemption" just completed by Jesus Christ? He had died redemptively; He had been resurrected from the dead; He had ascended into heaven. Everything was now in order for the cosmos to reap the benefits of His atoning work.

The Day of Pentecost meant dedication to the Lord. This is an appropriate analogy spiritually. The fullness of the Holy Spirit is always received in response to personal, total surrender.

Finally, Pentecost was a time of joy, radiance, festivity. The coming of the Holy Spirit always means gladness and radiance. The first response of the spectators to the joy of the Spirit-filled Christians was that they were "intoxicated with new wine" (Acts 2:13). Intoxication, even from illegitimate sources, has manifestations which the world calls joy. Paul exhorted Christians not to be intoxicated with wine but to be filled with the Spirit (Eph. 5:18). He likewise made reference to the joyfulness of the Spirit-filled experience: "The kingdom of God is not a matter of eating and drinking, but of righteousness, peace, and joy in the Holy Spirit" (Rom. 14:17).

WHERE WAS THE HOLY SPIRIT GIVEN?

Now note *where* the Holy Spirit was given. He was given, first of all, in the city. Contrast the coming of the Holy Spirit in the busy, bustling city with its teeming multitudes and frenzied activity with the Transfiguration of Jesus on a quiet, secluded mountain top.

Why the city? Here are some suggestions. The city is a place of concentrated problems. The Holy Spirit is related to life in all of its intricacies and perplexities. Jerusalem is the place where the disciples failed at the time of the Crucifixion. Stanley Jones writes:

> Jerusalem was the place of their failure . . . He was
> going to make the place of their greatest failure the place
> of their greatest success . . . The worst had been met and
> mastered. Henceforth they were ready for anything. If
> they could face Jerusalem and master it in His name,
> they could face anything and master it in His name![1]

It is a spiritual truth that we can be effective Christians
only if we are enabled through the power of the Holy Spirit
to succeed at those very places where, without Him, we
failed.

Why the city? The Great Commission must begin to be
fulfilled at the most difficult place. Think of calling Jerusalem to repentance and having results! John Newton, of
Olney, England, once prayed for "London grace." When
asked what was the meaning of this he replied, "By 'London
grace' I mean grace in a very high degree, grace to enable
one to live as a Christian even in London."

Furthermore, Jerusalem was the center of the highest
national and religious hopes of the Jewish people. The
coming of the Holy Spirit meant that God was establishing a
New Jerusalem, which was to transcend Jerusalem as they
knew it.

The Holy Spirit was also given in an upper room. This
has at least a double significance. In an upper room Jesus
instituted the Lord's Supper. He gave Himself to His
disciples. Now in an upper room on the day of Pentecost the
disciples were giving themselves totally to Him. The Upper
Room was also in a home, thus relating the Holy Spirit to
the everyday affairs of family living and relationships.

TO WHOM WAS THE HOLY SPIRIT GIVEN?

Consider also *to whom* the Spirit was given. He was
given to the 120 believers (the total number of Christian
believers at the time of the Ascension), not just to the
Twelve. He was given to women as well as to men. He was
not given to a particular sex or class or office, but to a person
as a person.

MEANS OF RECEPTION

The *means of the reception* of the Holy Spirit on the day of
Pentecost is significant. The disciples were not going
through a rite or ceremony or ordinance or sacrament when
the Spirit came. Rather, they were in the midst of a personal
spiritual experience—that of total surrender to Jesus Christ.
The Holy Spirit is received the moment that personal
surrender and faith are complete, whether it takes ten
seconds, ten minutes, ten hours, or ten days, as in the case of
the first Pentecost.

PHYSICAL PHENOMENA OF THE
HOLY SPIRIT

The day of Pentecost was characterized by certain
physical phenomena which accompanied the outpouring of the
Holy Spirit. There was the sound as of a rushing, mighty
wind which filled all the house where the disciples were
sitting (Acts 2:2). A tongue of fire was distributed (hovered
over the head of) to each of those waiting in the Upper
Room (Acts 2:3). After the Spirit-filled disciples went forth
from the Upper Room and mingled with the crowds on the
streets of Jerusalem, they were able to witness to them in
their own languages, languages with which the disciples
were unfamiliar (Acts 2:4–12).

E. Stanley Jones finds a spiritual significance in each
phenomenon. The sound as of a rushing, mighty wind
filling all the house signified the coming of the Holy Spirit as
a corporate experience. The group as a whole was to receive
the Spirit. The tongue of fire distributed to each one
indicated that each individual person would receive the
fullness of the Spirit. It was to be a personal as well as a
corporate experience.

The ability to communicate clearly in languages previously unknown was a symbol of the universality of the
Christian Gospel. The Great Commission instructed Christians to go into all the world and preach the Gospel to every
person of every race and nation and climate. Pentecost

marked the inauguration of the Christian missionary enterprise.

The physical phenomena of the first day of Pentecost
will not necessarily be repeated. They must be regarded as
"the scaffolding of Pentecost." The scaffolding is taken
down, but the newly constructed building remains. It is the
spiritual principle of Pentecost that is to abide.

WHAT IS PENTECOST?

Is Pentecost only a significant historical event or does it
mark a spiritual epoch? Is Pentecost only to be observed or is
it to be experienced? Is Pentecost only a monument or is it a
movement?

The experience of the apostles, the New Testament
church, and of Christian experience and activity through the
centuries reveals that Pentecost announces the possibility of
an epochal experience in redeeming grace and a new level in
Christian living. Pentecost is God's offer of Himself in total
adequacy to His children, made possible by the redeeming
work of His Son Jesus Christ. Pentecost is God's call to His
children to be purified inwardly and to be empowered for
witness in both the life and work to which He calls them. It
is God's affirmation of holiness as the norm of Christian
experience and life.

Pentecost is God's gift of Himself to His children. It
means that a Christian believer can have all of God that one
is capable of possessing. For illustration, the supply of sea
water is infinite. One's share of that sea water is determined
by the capacity of the receptacle used to draw water from the
sea. If a glass is used, then a glassful is all of the sea that
becomes available. If a bucket is used, then a bucketful
becomes the capacity of receptivity. If large tanks on
shipboard are filled from the sea, then these tanks will
contain all of the sea they are capable of holding. Just so, the
"amount" of God that a person possesses is determined by
the spiritual capacity of the person. Pentecost means that one
can have all of the spiritual power that one is capable of
receiving.

The religious movement known as Methodism has in the past been characterized by its emphasis upon this new level of spiritual experience and life through the Holy Spirit. John Wesley spent much of his ministry promulgating the doctrine of entire sanctification, scriptural holiness, Christian perfection. In his *Thoughts Upon Methodism* (1768) he wrote, "Christian perfection is the grand depositum which God has lodged with the people called Methodist; and for the sake of propagating this chiefly He appears to have raised us up."

In his *Plain Account Of Christian Perfection,* Wesley spoke of this experience in grace as "not so early as justification" and "not so late as death." It has often been referred to as "a second work of grace." Many do not understand the reason for the Wesleyan emphasis upon receiving the fullness of the Holy Spirit as a "second definite work of grace." The Wesleyan emphasis upon a second work of grace is modeled after the experience of the early disciples. They were converted before the day of Pentecost. On that day they were filled with the Holy Spirit.

For several reasons, Wesleyans believe that two definite works of grace are needed. First, the twofold nature of sin needs to be dealt with redemptively. Sin is both outward acts and inward nature. Initial salvation provides justification in relation to sins already committed and regeneration in effecting a new life of righteous conduct. Entire sanctification provides inner cleaning, thus dealing with the sin nature. That entire sanctification is different from and subsequent to initial salvation is the testimony of the saints across the Christian centuries. John Wesley wrote, "We do not know a single instance, in any place, of the person's receiving, in one and the same moment, remission of sins, the abiding witness of the Spirit, and a new, clean heart."

Second, the person seeking initial salvation is not aware of any need of a subsequent deeper experience of grace at that time. He craves forgiveness: "God be merciful to me a sinner." It is only after receiving forgiveness that the believer senses the inward struggle with the inherited sinful nature. Third, the person seeking initial salvation cannot meet the conditions of receiving the Holy Spirit in His fullness. The sinner is dead in trespasses and sins, and is capable only of confession. But the born-again Christian is able to present himself/herself as a "living sacrifice" unto God, an act that signifies total receptivity to the baptism of the Spirit.

Furthermore, the ministry of the Holy Spirit has a different redemptive focus in each of the two spiritual experiences of initial salvation and entire sanctification. In initial salvation the Holy Spirit performs a regenerating ministry. In entire sanctification the Holy Spirit effects a purifying work.

WHAT SANCTIFICATION IS NOT

We need to have an adequate understanding of the nature of sanctification as an epochal experience in the Christian believer's life. We look, first, at what entire sanctification is *not*.

1) It is *not* initial salvation. It is not the same as "regeneration," "justification," the "new birth." The disciples of Jesus were regenerated and justified persons before Pentecost. At that time they received a new experience in divine grace—they were filled with the Holy Spirit.

2) It is *not* any kind of mortal perfection. It does not restore Adamic perfection—the perfection of humankind before the Fall. It is not angelic perfection which is reserved for heavenly beings. It is not philosophical perfection which strives for a perfect human existence. It is not resurrection-life perfection of which Christians will partake after the resurrection of the body.

3) It is *not* exemption from temptation. Temptation is an inescapable part of the moral probation of our mortal existence. It will not cease until death. Nor can we expect freedom from ignorance, mistakes, and infirmities. Wesley wrote, "A man may be filled with pure love, and still be liable to mistake." Again he said, "The mind itself may be deeply distressed, may be exceedingly sorrowful, may be perplexed . . . while the heart cleaves to God by perfect love, and the will is wholly resigned to Him."

In this regard Wesley offers a meaningful insight into the nature of sin for which a person is accountable. He distinguishes between sin as "the voluntary transgression of a known law of God" and "involuntary transgression" which is the unintentional transgression of a law of God, presumably unknown. Because no one is free from "involuntary transgressions," Wesley said that he never would use the phrase "sinless perfection." However, he declared that "involuntary transgressions cannot properly be classified as sin, since the absence of intention carries with it no personal guilt."

4) It is *not* an experience in which it is impossible to sin. The removal of the possibility of sinning would dehumanize a finite person. Only God exists in such absolute impeccability. There is a radical difference between "not possible to sin" and "possible not to sin." Therefore, entire sanctification is not an experience from which a person cannot lapse. We hear Wesley again: "There is no such height or strength of holiness as is impossible to fall from." Robert Barclay wrote, "And thee remaineth always in some part a possibility of sinning where the mind doth not most diligently and watchfully attend unto the Lord."

5) It is *not* necessarily a replication of the outward phenomena of the first Christian Pentecost: the sound of a rushing, mighty wind; the distribution of a tongue of fire to each person; and the ability to bear witness to Christ in languages previously unknown. Some people through the years have made the mistake of thinking that we never experience the Spirit-filled life, that we are never entirely sanctified, unless some of these phenomena, or all of them, become a part of our own spiritual experience. This is a grossly mistaken notion.

6) It is *not* an unbalanced, eccentric kind of spiritual experience. The Spirit-filled life is not fanaticism. It is not sentimental weakness. It is not religious exclusiveness. It is not melancholy. It is not emaciation. It is not asceticism. God never called us to be holy in a "hole." "Eccentric" means "off-center." Some persons think—at least they seem so to think—that the more off-centered, unbalanced, and

abnormal they are, the more deeply spiritual they are. I recall visiting a church that had a large sign over the pulpit which read: "Jesus Christ is here. Don't be surprised at anything." But I must confess that if Jesus Christ were truly there, I might be surprised at some things if they should occur. Jesus had the Holy Spirit without measure, and He was the most balanced personality who ever lived. Spirit-filled Christianity is normal spiritual experience and activity.

7) It is *not* maturity of life. The crisis of being filled with the Holy Spirit is an experience of purity. Spiritual maturity is the ever-beckoning goal of the pure heart in the life that follows. Having one's heart made pure in love is but the beginning of a continuing life of "going on unto perfection." Purity leads to maturity. The late Archbishop William Temple spoke of the developing degrees of perfection. He illustrated it by noting the difference between the perfection of the immature child and the perfection of the more mature adult. But he pointed out that each is truly perfection at its own particular level of development.

WHAT SANCTIFICATION IS

So much then for what sanctification is *not*. We now deal with the other aspect of our subject: what *is* it? What happens when a person is "entirely sanctified"?

1) It *is* the crucifixion of the carnal mind. The carnal mind is the sin nature within us as the result of the Fall. It is inherited from generation to generation. It must be "crucified" if the Christian is to live victoriously over sin.

The carnal mind is not the self viewed as the essence of the human creation. Rather, it is the identification of the self with the sinful perversions of the subconscious mind. The self is to be crucified in the sense that sinful self-centeredness is destroyed, and the basic desires of the self are cleansed through the indwelling of the Holy Spirit.

St. Paul testified to such an experience: "I have been crucified with Christ and I no longer live, but Christ lives in me" (Gal. 2:20). Centuries later Robert Barclay wrote: " . . . The body of death and sin comes to be crucified and renewed . . . so as not to obey any suggestions or temptations of the evil one. . . ."

2) It *is* the disciplined control, under the influence of the Holy Spirit, of the human personality. It is the giving of ourselves to God as those who are alive from the dead, and the yielding of all our members to God as instruments of righteousness (Rom. 6:13).

The sanctified life does not rob us of our individual and differing human personalities. It does not mean exemption from constant Christian discipline. Rather, it does mean that the Holy Spirit, who is in complete control of our hearts and lives, directs and assists us in the necessary disciplining of every area of human personality.

3) It *is* the habitation of the Holy Spirit within us and our abiding in the Holy Spirit. It is reciprocal abiding: The Spirit in us and we in the Spirit. The blacksmith thrusts his iron into the fire. After a while it becomes red hot. Then it is difficult to tell whether the iron is in the fire or the fire is in the iron.

Such abiding in the Spirit brings new dimensions to the Christian life—the dimension of purity and the dimension of power. The Spirit-filled individual is made adequate by the Holy Spirit both to be and to do what God intends.

4) It *is* perfect love. This is the term that perhaps best describes what Wesley had in mind when he enjoined such an experience upon "the people called Methodist." Wesley's own descriptions of the experience are illuminating and deeply meaningful: "This it is to be a perfect man . . . even to have a heart so all-flaming with the love of God . . . as continually to offer up every thought, word, and work, as a spiritual sacrifice, acceptable to God through Christ."

It is to be inwardly, and outwardly devoted to God. It is loving God with all the heart, mind, soul, and strength. This implies that no wrong temper, none contrary to love remains in the soul: and that all the thoughts, words, and actions are governed by pure love.

5) It *means* to be filled with Jesus Christ. Jesus said, "I will send another comforter." He was going to send another Person just like Himself—the Holy Spirit. We read: "If

anyone does not have the Spirit of Christ, he does not belong to Christ" (Rom. 8:9). If we are possessed by the Holy Spirit, we will be like Christ.

We need to keep in mind that it is possible to be under the influence of a spirit which isn't the Holy Spirit, even though we are tempted to think that all "spirit experiences" are holy ones. A young artist tried to duplicate the masterpiece of his master. He used everything that was his master's—his studio, his canvas, his brushes, his paints, his model. However, upon viewing the young man's work, a fellow artist responded, "You have everything that is your masters' except his spirit."

6) It *is* the manifestation of the fruit of the Spirit in one's life. In Galatians 5:22–23, St. Paul identifies the results of the Spirit's presence in the believer as love, joy, peace, longsuffering, gentleness, goodness, truth, meekness, self-control. Three fruits are for God to feed on—love, goodness, faith. Three are for others to feed on—joy, gentleness, meekness. And three are for one's self to feed on—peace, longsuffering, self-control.

7) The Spirit-filled life *is* the Christian's daily life lived under the influence of the active ministry of the Holy Spirit. In Romans 8, Paul outlines at least thirteen ministries of the Holy Spirit promised to those in whom He dwells: liberation (v. 2), indwelling (v. 9), identification (v. 9), resurrection (v. 11), healing (v. 11), crucifixion (v. 13), guidance (v. 14), acceptance (v. 15), assurance (v. 16), warranty (v. 23), enabling (v. 26), intercession (vv. 26–27), revelation (vv. 28–39).

The question is often raised: What does the fullness of the Spirit do for a Christian which regeneration has not already accomplished? Here again the early Christians are our model. There were radical transformations in their lives after Pentecost.

First, look at early Christians corporately. At the time of the crucifixion of Jesus they went into hiding. They were behind closed doors because they were afraid. But after the Holy Spirit came upon them, everything was changed. No longer were they afraid to witness to their Lord. He was alive—and so were they! They went everywhere preaching the Gospel. And they did so with boldness. They counted it a privilege to suffer for their faith.

Now look at Peter who is representative of the others. He denied his Lord three times. He was in hiding. He had trouble believing that Jesus had risen from the dead. In his frustration he was tempted to return to his fishing. But something happened to Peter on Pentecost. He stood straight on that day and proclaimed the gospel of a crucified and risen Lord to a mighty multitude in the face of hostile Jews. Fear and cowardice had vanished from Peter's life. He followed his Master faithfully all the way to his own cross. Perhaps as tradition says, he was crucified head downward.

What difference does Pentecost make to the Christian? The fullness of the Holy Spirit adds purity and power.

Spiritual power really means adequacy. The person who is Spirit-filled is made adequate by the Holy Spirit to be and become and do what God intends. We need power for holy living, day by day. We need power to minister effectively in the place where God has placed us. We need power to witness to Jesus Christ. We need power in order to mature spiritually. The power of the Spirit is an energy which forces a way through to a new level of achievement.

HOW DOES THE CHRISTIAN RECEIVE THE HOLY SPIRIT?

The Gift of the Holy Spirit is for every Christian believer. How, then does the Christian receive the Holy Spirit in His fullness? Here are five steps:

1) Believe Christ's promise and Christ's imperative about the Holy Spirit.

2) Confess your need of the inward purity and power which the Holy Spirit provides.

3) Make a total surrender of yourself. Invite the Holy Spirit to come into every part of your being—into your mind, your emotions, your spirit, your soul, your body, your nerves, all your bodily processes—into all of you.

4) In response to your total surrender, accept by faith what the Holy Spirit wants to do for you.

5) Enter into an abiding covenant of obedience with your Lord. Say, "Now all of me, Lord is yours, *forever.*"

I knelt as a high school sophomore at an altar in a small Methodist church in southern New Jersey to seek the fullness of the Spirit. That evening, actually in my mind, I laid two bundles upon the altar rail. I can see them now. One was a small bundle and it bore the label "all that I know." As a sophomore in high school, I really did not know much. The other bundle was labeled "all that I do not know." It was so big that I wondered if it would fit in under the ceiling of the sanctuary. I realized that night that I was giving God my all—"all that I know" and "all that I do not know." I could not give Him any more.

Many times since that night in my boyhood church, the divine hand has reached into the bundle which was then marked "all that I do not know," and pulled out something, now to be known. Then I have been confronted with the soul-penetrating question: "Did you really mean what you said that night? Are you willing to consecrate this also? Can this now be placed in the other bundle 'all that I know?'"

I believe that each time I have been able to say "Yes, Lord." By His grace, I have endeavored to live in a continuing covenant of obedience to Christ.

E. Stanley Jones visited the cathedral at Copenhagen to see Thorwaldsen's exquisite status of Christ, which dominated the entire cathedral. As he approached the work, a Danish friend whispered, "You will not be able to see His face unless you kneel at His feet." It was true, for Christ was standing with outstretched arms looking at those at His feet. Dr. Jones knelt at His feet, and lo, Christ's face looked into his. How true in relation to spiritual experience! You cannot really see Christ until you bend the knee to Him, until you surrender to Him. You cannot receive the Holy Spirit in His fullness until you consecrate yourself totally to Him.

How may a person be sure that he has received the Holy Spirit in His fullness, that the Holy Spirit has taken total possession and abides within? In a philosophy class during a college revival, this same question was asked the professor. Without saying a word, he rose from his desk, walked down the aisle, out of the classroom, and closed the door after him. You can imagine how bewildered the class was because of such behavior. In a moment or two, the classroom door opened, the professor entered the room, proceeded down the aisle to the slightly raised platform to his desk, and sat down. When he was situated comfortably, he looked up at the class and asked, "Did I come in?" Then after a few seconds pause he commented, "You will know just as surely when the Holy Spirit comes into your life in His fullness." Thus the Holy Spirit makes spiritual experience real to our consciences.

Wesley also declared that the Spirit-filled experience is attested to by the manifestation of the fruit of the Spirit. There is not only the witness within, but also the witness without.

What happened at Pentecost? The first disciples received the gift of the fullness of the Holy Spirit. Pentecost has been happening all across the Christian centuries. God wants Pentecost to continue to recur—in the experience of every Christian and in the life of every local church.

3 | *THE HOLY SPIRIT'S WORK IN YOU AND ME*

> When the Counselor comes, whom I will send . . . He will. . . .
>
> *(John 15:26; 16:13–15)*

The coming of the Holy Spirit in His fullness was both a corporate and a personal experience.

Most of the teachings of Jesus about the Holy Spirit during the closing days of His ministry dealt with the individual Christian. The ministry of the Holy Spirit to the individual can be viewed in four main areas: enlightenment, enlivening, enrichment, empowering. "I will ask the Father, and he will give you another Counselor . . . —the Spirit of truth . . . [who] will teach you all things and will remind you of everything I have said to you" (John 14:16–17, 26). "The Spirit gives life" (John 6:63). "The fruit of the Spirit is. . . ." (Gal. 5:22). "You will receive power when the Holy Spirit comes on you" (Acts 1:8).

THE HOLY SPIRIT ENLIGHTENS

To enlighten means to give intellectual or spiritual light: to instruct, inform, and to edify.

The Holy Spirit is the Spirit of Truth. He is a personal teacher. He is the Revealer of truth in contrast to falsehood. The Spirit makes a person conscious that it is the truth which He is revealing. To the soul the Spirit makes the light light, and the truth truth. The spiritual knowledge that the Holy Spirit imparts is always within the parameters of the teachings of Christ. The Spirit is not a source of independent revelation, only the revelation of Christ.

The Spirit does this through a two-fold process: teaching and testimony. There is an operation of the Spirit that is educative, ever extending the area of spiritual understanding. The Spirit is the living Divine Teacher who works in us a progressive understanding of the contents of the truth embodied in Christ.

But the illumination wrought by the Spirit is not only teaching; it is also testimony. Not only does the Spirit bring to the Christian's remembrance all that Christ said (John 14:26), but He also continually bears witness to Christ (John 15:26). Through both His teaching and testimony the joyous assurance of faith becomes the Spirit's gift to the Christian believer.

We need the Holy Spirit to help us sort out our "certainties." It is so easy for us to label our personal opinions, even our prejudices, as certainties. But actually we can be certain of only that which is truth. We need the Spirit to inspire and guide us into those experiences that deepen our sense of certainty.

The Spirit interprets truth and helps a person to apply the truth to all relationships. The truth revealed by Jesus Christ is relevant to all issues and circumstances of life. It is universal truth, timeless truth. But without the Spirit the Christian is helpless to understand all the applications of such truth.

We are to have "the mind of Christ" in all things. What is "the mind of Christ" in relation to divorce? to abortion? to genetic engineering? to euthanasia? to capitalistic profits? to capital punishment? to war? nuclear weapons? Of course, there are no easy answers. But the thoughtful Christian is not willing to close his mind to these perplexing, pressing issues of contemporary life. With the help of the Spirit, light from the teachings of Jesus is forthcoming, and the Christian finds himself enlightened and guided.

The truth revealed by the Holy Spirit is always

edifying. It leads to spiritual security (John 14:18–21). It results in inward cleansing (John 15:3), peace (John 14:27), and joy (John 15:11). It means effectiveness in prayer (John 15:7) and fruitfulness in ministry (John 15:5).

As a part of His ministry of enlightenment the Holy Spirit witnesses to the reality of spiritual experience. One is reminded of Paul's words in Romans 8:15–16 about this ministry of the Holy Spirit: "By him we cry, *Abba*, Father. The Spirit himself testifies with our spirit that we are God's children."

One of the distinctive Wesleyan emphases has been upon this witness of the Spirit. Early in his ministry John Wesley proclaimed the doctrine of spiritual assurance. He defined it in these words:

> By the witness of the Spirit I mean an inward impression on the soul, whereby the Spirit of God immediately and directly witnesses to my spirit, that I am a child of God; that Jesus Christ hath loved me and given Himself for me; that all my sins are blotted out, and I, even I, am reconciled to God (from the sermon "The Witness of the Spirit").

There are at least four significant implications in Wesley's definition. The witness of the Spirit is not the result of reasoning. It is not a mere emotional feeling. Rather, it is a supernatural impression upon a person's spiritual consciousness effected through the personal working of the Holy Spirit. And it must be kept in mind that the Holy Spirit always witnesses to a present state of grace, never to a future one.

Wesley held that the witness of the Spirit is valid for every epochal experience of redeeming grace. The Spirit bears witness to the actuality of the new birth in one's experience. Likewise, the Spirit bears witness to both the crisis experience of entire sanctification and to the continuing process of sanctification in one's life. (See Wesley's *A Plain Account of Christian Perfection*.)

Wesley never considered this doctrine of the witness of the Spirit as either the original discovery or sole possession of the Methodists. On July 9, 1766, he included the following lines in a letter to Samuel Furly:

> Seventeen or eighteen years ago, after much searching of the Scriptures and mature deliberation, I wrote my thoughts concerning the witness of God's Spirit and the witness of our own spirit. I have not yet seen any reason to change my judgment on either of these subjects; rather I am confirmed therein more and more both by the living and dying children of God. And this is no peculiarity of the Methodists. Many I have found in various parts both of Great Britain and Ireland (to say nothing of Holland, Germany, and America) who enjoyed that immediate witness before they had any sort of connexion with the Methodists or any knowledge either of their persons or writings. . . .

On November 23, 1654, Blaise Pascal, eminent French mathematician and philosopher, had a profound religious experience that led him to devote the remainder of his life principally to religious activities. He wrote the following memorial of it, had a copy of it sewn into his clothing, and wore it to keep himself reminded of the event.

> The year of grace 1654, Monday the twenty-third of November, St. Clement's Day . . . from about half past ten in the evening until about half-an-hour after midnight—FIRE. God of Abraham, God of Isaac, God of Jacob, not of the philosophers and the learned. Certainty; certainty; feeling; joy; peace.[1]

An aspect of the ministry of enlightenment, sometimes ignored or bypassed, is the ministry of the discernment, one of the gifts of the Spirit (1 Cor. 12:10). Simply speaking, discernment is the ability to identify reality in spiritual matters, to know when Christ is speaking. The Scriptures speak of testing the spirits, to discover whether they are of God (I John 4:1).

James C. Fenhagen, writes in *Ministry and Solitude:* "For growth in the Spirit involves both our ability to see where the Spirit is leading us and our capacity to identify the presence of evil that stands in the way. Discernment is the gift of prophetic vision that moves Christian spirituality from sentiment to reality."[2]

Discernment means that with the help of God it is possible to distinguish the presence of the good and the bad. Ignatius of Loyola, Spanish founder of the Society of Jesus (Jesuits), in his *Spiritual Exercises* comments that the distinction is clear to those spiritually sensitive: "When persons are advancing from good to better, the touch of the good angel is soft, light, and gentle, like a drop of water being absorbed by a sponge. The touch of the evil angel is rough, accompanied by noise and disturbance, like a drop of water hitting a rock" (Ibid., p. 135).

Even though the process of discernment can never be stereotyped, at the heart of it is a universal criterion: Is the spiritual experience, the revelation, the guidance one claims to have been given, like Jesus?

The Holy Spirit also helps us to identify our spiritual gifts. Paul writes, "We have not received the spirit of the world but the Spirit who is from God, that we may understand what God has freely given us" (1 Cor. 2:12).

THE HOLY SPIRIT ENLIVENS

The Holy Spirit not only enlightens, He also enlivens. To enliven means to make alive, to invigorate, to energize.

Speaking generally, the Holy Spirit keeps alive a person's consciousness of the spiritual world. We were created with an innate spiritual consciousness, but how many times this has been dulled and desensitized! Yet in one way or another the Holy Spirit keeps at least a spark of it alive. This is a ministry of the Holy Spirit to all people in general, but the Christian is not exempt from temptations to worldliness in contrast with spirituality. Recall the lines of Isaac Watts:

> Look how we grovel here below,
>   Fond of these earthly toys;
> Our souls, how heavily they go,
>   To reach eternal joys.

Centering our attention upon the enlivening ministry of the Holy Spirit of Christians, we begin by recognizing that the Holy Spirit is the source of all spiritual life. We are "born of the Spirit." Becoming a Christian is through a new birth (John 3:5–6). This new birth is "not of natural descent, nor of human decision or a husband's will, but born of God" (John 1:13).

The Holy Spirit makes this experience alive and real to the believer. As Charles Wesley wrote about the Holy Spirit, "No man can truly say that Jesus is the Lord, unless Thou take the veil away, and breathe the Living Word."

The immediate result of the new birth is the quickening of a person's total personality. Paul writes about this "new creation": "Therefore, if anyone is in Christ, he is a new creation; the old has gone, the new has come" (2 Cor. 5:17). Another translation describes the "new" in these words: "All things become new" (KJV). Everything about the person who has been "born of the Spirit" is renewed, revitalized. Every faculty, every ability is cleansed and heightened by the activity of the Holy Spirit within.

The Holy Spirit influences all our natural powers, strengthens them, brings them up to their highest, and gives them a "plus." The natural is only at its best when it is reinforced by the supernatural. It becomes possible for ordinary persons to do extraordinary things. The Holy Spirit does not reduce people to their zero. He raises them to their zenith. The Holy Spirit is the Strong One creating the strong ones.

Paul talks about such a transformation through the Spirit: "Do not conform any longer to the pattern of this world, but be transformed by the renewing of your mind. Then you will be able to test and approve what God's will is—his good, pleasing and perfect will" (Rom. 12:2). It is significant that the Greek work "nous" ($\nu o \acute{o} \varsigma$) which Paul uses for "mind" here refers to the mind's faculties of perceiving, understanding, feeling, judging, and determining. It is a reference to the faculty to recognizing goodness and of hating evil.

The Holy Spirit also quickens the Word of God to the

believer. Through the Spirit, the believer becomes alive to the transcendence of God's Word and to a spiritual understanding of its content. Those not born of the Spirit are dead to God's Word. The Old Testament prophets spoke of such individuals as "having ears, but not hearing; having eyes, but not seeing" (Jer. 5:21; Ezek. 12:2).

The apostle Paul makes it clear that spiritual things are discerned only by the spiritually minded. He writes in 1 Corinthians 2:13–14:

> This is what we speak, not in words taught us by human wisdom but in words taught by the Spirit, expressing spiritual truths in spiritual words. The man without the Spirit does not accept the things that come from the Spirit of God, for they are foolishness to him, and he cannot understand them, because they are spiritually discerned.

This is what Jesus meant when He exhorted His hearers, "He who has ears, let him hear" (Matt. 11:15; 13:9, 43; Mark 4:9, 23; 7:16; Luke 8:8; 14:35).

The Holy Spirit quickens the Christian to participate in the redemptive ministries assigned by Christ. Particularly does he quicken the Christian to witness to him and to perform deeds of loving kindness and service in his name. He makes the Christian zealous and enthusiastic about the work of Christ. The Greek word translated *enthusiasm* means to be packed full of God.

The Holy Spirit is the secret of a never-failing supply of spiritual energy for the Christian. The Spirit is never to be quenched; the fire of the Spirit is never to be suppressed or dampened or put out (1 Thess. 5:19). Then the Christian will be "aglow with the Spirit" (Rom. 12:11, RSV) and need never to be indicted for "losing one's first love" (Rev. 2:4).

Isaac Watts sensed the quickening power of the Holy Spirit when he penned these lines:

> Come, Holy Spirit, heavenly Dove,
> With all thy quickening powers;
> Kindle a flame of sacred love
> In these cold hearts of ours.

What about those times when even professing Christians seem to appear spiritually dead and devoid of spiritual zeal? Certainly a part of the Spirit's enlivening ministry is that of revival and renewal. What else does Ezekiel's vision of the Valley of Dry Bones mean (Ezek. 37:1–14)? God asked the prophet this question: "Can these bones live?" (v. 3) God answered His own question both by activity and word. He called upon the Spirit to breathe upon them, and they lived (vv. 9–10). God summarized it all when He told the prophet, "I will put my Spirit in you, and you will live" (v. 14).

The resurrected Christ gave the same promise of revival and renewal to the church at Laodicea, spoken of in the book of the Revelation (3:14–20):

> I know your deeds, that you are neither cold nor hot . . .
> I counsel you to buy from me gold refined in the fire, so
> you can become rich; and white clothes to wear, so you
> can cover your shameful nakedness; and salve to put on
> your eyes, so you can see . . . be earnest and repent.
> Here I am! I stand at the door and knock. If anyone hears
> my voice and opens the door, I will come in and eat
> with him, and he with me.

The Holy Spirit quickens the Christian to believe the promises of Christ and appropriate them. Some folks have trouble in believing; others believe but have difficulty in appropriating. The quickening ministry of the Holy Spirit deals with both of these areas.

The Holy Spirit convinces the Christian that the promises of Christ are authentic: "Come to me . . . and I will give you rest" (Matt. 11:28); "Whoever drinks the water that I give him will never thirst" (John 4:14); "He who comes to me will never go hungry" (John 6:35); "Ask whatever you wish, and it will be given you" (John 15:7); "My peace I give you" (John 14:27); "Anyone who has faith will do what I have been doing. He will do even greater things than these" (John 14:12); "He who lives and believes in me will never die" (John 11:26).

These are but a few of the promises of Christ. Do we

believe them? The Holy Spirit quickens us into confident belief. Are we appropriating them? The Holy Spirit wants to quicken us into appropriating faith.

Furthermore, the Holy Spirit causes the Christian to be sensitive to the meaning of contemporary events. At one point in His ministry, Jesus rebuked the Pharisees and Sadducees for being insensitive to "the signs of the times." He said to them: "When evening comes, you say, 'It will be fair weather, for the sky is red,' and in the morning, 'Today it will be stormy, for the sky is red and overcast.' You know how to interpret the appearance of the sky, but you cannot interpret the signs of the times" (Matt. 16:2–3).

One is reminded of the way in which the Holy Spirit caused Peter, a radical, self-satisfied Jew, to become sensitive to the needs of the Gentiles for salvation. The story is told in the tenth chapter of Acts. The bottom line of it all is found in Peter's report to the leaders at Jerusalem after he made his divinely appointed visit to the home of Cornelius. Among other things he declared that he had become convinced that what God has cleansed no one must call common or unclean and that God is giving the gift of salvation to the Gentiles as well as to the Jews (Acts 11:1–18).

For Christianity to be relevant in any age, Spirit-filled Christians must be sensitized to the meaning of contemporary happenings. Once, on a tour to Alaska, we were impressed with the suddenness and intensity of the tides, which cover the land in a very short time. Our guide commented: "If you live here and want to survive you must know your tides." This can be applied spiritually in a very real way. The church must know the "tides" of contemporary life and offer with insight and confidence the never-failing relevance of the Gospel.

One of the neglected areas in the enlivening ministry of the Holy Spirit is that of the inspiration of the Spirit. I am not referring primarily to the Spirit's inspiration of the Holy Scriptures. Evangelicals have always believed that the Bible, both in its original writings and in the collection of the writings, is not mere human accomplishment but the work of the Holy Spirit. We are considering, rather, the Spirit's ministry of inspiration in relation to the individual Christian.

What is meant by "inspiration"? Basically "to inspire" means to "breathe into." The Spirit's inspiration is the breath of God's Spirit blowing directly upon a person.

Inspiration operates upon the mind, the emotions, and the will of a person. In relation to the mind, inspiration means the infusion of ideas. There can be the infusion of ideas by direct supernatural influences. Elihu, in one of his conversations with the patriarch Job, spoke of the inspiration of the Almighty giving understanding to the spirit of man (Job 32:8). We become aware of the inspiration of the Holy Spirit in the writing of hymns, spiritual songs, poems, and books, and in the envisioning and implementation of programs for the expansion of God's kingdom.

What about the so-called secular areas of life? Does the inspiration of the Holy Spirit extend to these areas as well as to the strictly spiritual areas? Actually, the Holy Spirit dissolves the assumed dichotomy between the spiritual and the secular.

In a sermon I heard E. Stanley Jones preach when I was a college student, he said, "We must naturalize the spiritual and spiritualize the natural so that we will not know where the spiritual ends and the natural begins, or where the natural ends and the spiritual begins."

The inspiration of the Holy Spirit extends to all the legitimate areas of human experience. Great "secular" poems and books have been inspired. Great productions of art bear the mark of God's inspiration. The great composer, Haydn, remarked in response to accolades of praise that were being heaped upon his composition, *The Creation,* "Not to me, but to Him; from Him it all comes."

Great discoveries in every branch of science must certainly have been inspired. George Washington Carver asked God, "Mr. Creator, tell me what I can do with the peanut in order to help my people." What about Louis Pasteur, whose discoveries led to the process of the pasteurization of milk; and Jonas Salk and Albert Sabin and their discovery of a vaccine against polio? Was there not divine inspiration upon human minds in all this scientific research?

What about leaders in government who have contributed so significantly to moral and social betterment? Were not William Wilberforce and Abraham Lincoln inspired to lead the fight against human slavery? Was not Martin Luther King inspired in his crusade for human rights? And so on.

The inspiration of the Holy Spirit upon Christians is often effected through the imagination. The writer of the epistle to the Hebrews talks about the use of the imagination in helping us bear one another's burdens: "Remember those in prison, as if you were their fellow prisoners, and those who are mistreated as if you yourselves were suffering" (13:3).

But the inspiration of the Holy Spirit is not limited to the mind; it extends also to the emotions. When the emotions are inspired, they are animated, cheered, and exhilarated. We are gaining a new appreciation both of the importance of wholesome emotions as the support system of the human personality and the relationship between the emotions and the mind.

The inspiration of the Holy Spirit operates upon the wills of people through spiritual dedication which expresses itself through the will. In turn, such exercise of the will sustains and enhances the life of one's spirit.

There are times when one is inspired to pray for another person, or for a situation, without the mind's knowledge of any particular need of prayer. Christian biography and autobiography are replete with illustrations of such Spirit-inspired intercessions. Once while recovering from a hospitalization, I received a letter from an esteemed friend telling me that he had been strangely yet insistently called to prayer on my behalf. He knew nothing of my special needs when he was called to prayer. Truly the Spirit called him to intercession on my behalf.

The inspiration of the Holy Spirit is also manifest in the performance of special acts of Christian ministry exactly at the time when they were needed, without any factual appeals from those in need. So many times Christians have been inspired to write letters of encouragement or make visits upon those who needed special help. Repeatedly financial help has been sent by people inspired by the Spirit just at the time when it was needed most. The things I am talking about in this regard were not initiated primarily by human volition. Rather, they were inspirations of the Spirit who knows all about all situations and who moves upon the wills of those who are sensitive to Him.

How many times Christians have borne witness to the fact that they have been enable to perform deeds, or to continue in some course of spiritual ministry for a special period of time because of something far greater than mere human ability or endurance! There was the touch of the supernatural, the Spirit upon them—truly an inspiration, an in-breathing.

A final enlivening ministry of the Holy Spirit is His quickening of hope. He Himself is a token of hope. "The Spirit is God's mark of ownership on you, a guarantee that the Day will come when God will set you free" (Eph. 4:30, TEV). "[God] has given us the Holy Spirit in our hearts as the guarantee of all that He has in store for us" (2 Cor. 1:22, TEV).

One of the ministries of the Holy Spirit as promised by Jesus is in relation to the future. "He will declare to you the things that are to come" (John 16:13, RSV). But this ministry deals with more than facts; it relates to spirit. He is the Creator and Sustainer of hope. Interspersed with Jesus' discussion of the Spirit's ministry, as recorded in the closing chapters of the Gospel According to John, are His promises about "peace," "untroubled hearts," "good cheer," "joy," "greater works," "overcoming the wicked one," "overcoming the world."

An Old Testament prophet spoke of "the people of God" as "prisoners of hope" (Zech. 9:12). John Henry Jowett spoke of the Early Christians as possessing "apostolic optimism." Paul said that we are "saved by hope" (Rom. 8:24). Throughout the Christian centuries the Holy Spirit has quickened the hope of Christians in the final glorious outcome of all things and in the triumphant consummation of all God's redemptive plans.

THE HOLY SPIRIT ENRICHES

The Holy Spirit also wants to enrich the quality of our spiritual experiences and to make possible a higher level of Christian living. To enrich is to make finer in quality, to supply with an abundance of anything desirable.

When we speak of the enriching ministry of the Holy Spirit we are thinking primarily of the quality of one's life, of the character of the Christian, of the manifestation of Christ-like personality. How important this is!

Dr. David L. Thompson once reported on a study made by Ronald Kelly comparing a Wesleyan group with a Christian Reformed group. The study asked them to analyze and recommend a course of action in certain case dilemmas presented to them. The study showed no significant differences in the responses. The Wesleyans verbalized more about "loving and caring for others"; but the study could not say whether they were more apt to *implement* love than the Reformed group. Dr. Thompson commented:

> I must add a reluctant conclusion from my own experience with the denomination of which I am a part. After fifteen years of ordained ministry, I confess seeing little evidence at *any* level of the church that we produce as a whole persons of loftier Christian character, more authentic devotion to Christ, more penetrating moral perception or more courageous moral action, more apt to love the Lord their God with all their heart, soul, mind and strength than any other group of persons who claim to take the Gospel seriously.[3]

But the Holy Spirit wants to enrich the moral and spiritual character of our spiritual experience and thus to make Spirit-filled Christians "different." There are three areas of the Spirit's work which contribute to such personal enrichment.

First, the exponents of the experience of the fullness of

the Holy Spirit have always claimed that in some degree or another the Spirit-filled heart is cleansed from the domination of the sin nature. In describing what Pentecost means, even for the Gentiles, Peter said to the Council at Jerusalem: "[God gave] the Holy Spirit to them, just as he did to us. He made no distinction between us and them, for he purified their hearts by faith" (Acts 15:8–9).

Such cleansing is difficult to define, but it certainly has such spiritual manifestations as single-mindedness, the crucifixion of the carnal mind, and the total domination of love. Jesus talked about single-mindedness in the Sermon on the Mount. "Blessed are the pure in heart, for they will see God" (Matt. 5:8). The Greek word here translated "pure" means unmixed, unadulterated. It is the word for wine that has not been watered down. When used of glass, it indicates clear glass. What this beatitude designates as purity of heart is single-mindedness. The person who is pure in heart is clear and unmixed in purpose. Søren Kierkegaard, the Danish theologian, said that "purity of heart is to will one thing." Martin Luther wrote, "What is meant by a pure heart is this: one that is watching and pondering what God says and replacing its own ideas with the will of God." It is inevitable that those who single-mindedly submit all of life to what God says and wills shall "see God."

Purity is the cleansing of the heart from inner conflict, inner division, inner unrighteousness. It is the crucifixion of the carnal nature, the destruction of that self-centeredness which binds the self to evil inclinations. Purity makes possible the growth of positive emotions. Purity provides the single-mindedness of love.

John Wesley, the outstanding exponent of this deeper experience, describes sanctification:

> Always remember the essence of Christian holiness is simplicity and purity; one design, one desire; entire devotion to God. (Farewell Sermon at Epworth, 1735)
>
> It is all the mind which was in Christ, enabling us to walk as Christ walked. It is a renewal of the heart in the

whole image of God, the full likeness of Him that created it. (*A Plain Account of Christian Perfection,* 1766)

This it is to be a perfect man . . . even to have a heart so all-flaming with the love of God . . . as continually to offer up every thought, word, and work, as a spiritual sacrifice, acceptable to God through Christ.

This implies that no wrong temper, none contrary to love remains in the soul; and that all the thoughts, words, and actions are governed by pure love. (The Sermon "Christian Perfection")

The refiner's fire purges out all that is contrary to love, and that many times by a pleasing smart. (From a letter to Walter Churchey, February 21, 1771)

I believe this perfection is always wrought in the soul by a simple act of faith; consequently in an instant.

But I believe a gradual work, both preceding and following that instant. ("Brief Thoughts on Christian Perfection," January 27, 1767)

Perfect love is the goal and possible realization of the Christian life. It is by the work of this gracious Spirit that suddenly, in an instant, man's bent to sinning is replaced by perfect love. (The Sermon "The Repentance of Believers")

In summary, purity relates to every part of a person's being:

PURE WILL—To will one thing, the glory of God

PURE MIND—"Let this mind be in you which was also in Christ."

PURE EMOTIONS—Positive emotions, bound together and undergirded by love

PURE BODY—The body as the temple of the Holy Spirit

Purity means a new attachment of the self to godliness and the good. Purity may be likened to a snow-white lily growing in a polluted, dusty location. The grit and the grime of the atmosphere will not adhere to it. It remains radiant and unstained. Should not our hearts have the same characteristic? We cannot help that we live in a world full of evil. But God's grace can keep us so clean and unspotted that though we touch sin on every side, it will not cling to us.

The enriching ministry of the Holy Spirit is seen, furthermore, in the manifestation of the fruit of the Spirit. When we speak of the fruit of the Spirit we are dealing with a spiritual universal. Whereas the gifts of the Spirit are for divinely chosen individuals, every Spirit-filled person is to manifest the fruit of the Spirit. This is the real confirmation of the reality of the Spirit-filled life. The judgment is to be made according to the fruit test rather than the gift test. In spiritual experience, truth and character are more important than signs and miracles. In an orderly universe every effect must have an appropriate and adequate cause. This is just as true in the spiritual realm as in the physical world.

St. Paul points out that when the flesh, unsanctified flesh, the sinful self, is dominant in one's life and controls it, the effects are inevitably the works of the flesh as listed in Galatians 5:19–21. But the opposite is just as true. When the Holy Spirit controls one's life, the result is the fruit of the Spirit—love, joy, peace, longsuffering, gentleness, faith, meekness, self-control (Gal. 5:22–23).

On the basis of Paul's description of the fruit of the Spirit, let us create a composite picture of the Spirit-filled person. Here is a person with a loving heart, for the fruit of the Spirit is love. This person has a singing voice, for the fruit of the Spirit is joy. The brow is not ruffled, for the fruit of the Spirit is peace. There are broad shoulders, for the fruit of the Spirit is patience. The hand is gentle and the face is honest, for the fruit of the Spirit is kindness and goodness. This person has a confident mind, for the fruit of the Spirit is faith. This person manifests contentment, for the fruit of the Spirit is meekness. The Spirit-filled person walks with guarded step, for the fruit of the Spirit is discipline.

Likewise, this passage on the fruit of the Spirit reveals the necessary process of Christian maturity. One of the translations speaks of "the harvest of the Spirit." The harvest in the physical world has to grow in accordance with the laws of nature. Just so, in the spiritual realm the harvest is dependent upon the process of maturity in accordance with spiritual laws.

Paul gives us a key in relation to our cooperation with the Holy Spirit in the process of Christian maturity. Look at the first aspect of the fruit of the Spirit—love. Now look at the last mentioned aspect—discipline. Is not the secret of one's growth in grace dependent upon the disciplined responses of love? Dr. Paul S. Rees suggested that the fruit of the Spirit is actually love, in its manifold manifestations:

> Joy is the gladness of love. It is love in relation to the world. Peace is the quietness of love. It is love in relation to one's self. Longsuffering is the patience of love. It is love in relation to suffering. Gentleness is the graciousness of love. It is love in human relationships. Goodness is the character of love. It is love in relation to morality. Faith is the confidence of love. It is love in relation to the totality of life. Meekness is the humility of love. It is love in relation to God. Discipline is the self-control of love. It is love in constant training.

Purity, cleansing, the fruit of the Spirit! But there is even more. The Spirit makes possible the full potential of enriching spiritual growth. The Holy Spirit is the active agent in the continuing process of spiritual formation (growth in grace).

What do we mean by spiritual formation? "Spiritual" has to do with one's sense of the sacred. Spiritual formation, therefore, is the lived process through which one becomes able to identify for one's self what is ultimately sacred, and to devote one's self increasingly to the supreme values in human existence. It is the opening of the human personality in every dimension to the work of the Holy Spirit. It is the forming of Christ in a human being.

My favorite one-sentence definition of spiritual formation is this: "The journey of the total person toward wholeness." Scripturally, spiritual formation is growth in the grace and the knowledge of the Lord Jesus Christ. Theologically, spiritual formation is the process by which the image of Christ is formed in us. Psychologically, spiritual formation is the pursuit of maturity.

Spiritual formation is imperative for every Christian. There are many reasons for this:

1. Spiritual formation is imperative so that the Christian may fulfill the divine ideal of Christlikeness. John Wesley said, "The imitation of Christ is our chief worship."

2. Spiritual formation is imperative in order to conform to the law of all life: grow or perish. There is nothing static in life; life is dynamic. It either grows or dies. Just so, spiritual life either progresses or regresses. There are no vital plateaus in Christian experience.

3. Spiritual formation is imperative because of the nature of the Christian life in this present world—a continuing struggle with evil and the necessity of finding the secret to overcome evil. Paul wrote, "We are not fighting against human beings, but against the wicked spiritual forces in the heavenly world, the rulers, authorities and cosmic powers of this dark age" (Eph. 6:12, TEV).

4. Spiritual formation is imperative in order to discover one's authentic self. Far too many people go through life wearing masks. We have to discover our true selves if we are ever to reach the full potential of our selfhood. Spiritual formation brings a person face to face with spiritual reality and hence with himself.

5. Spiritual formation is imperative in order to establish and maintain a proper balance between the emotions and the mind in spiritual experience. The romanticist deals only with emotions; the rationalist deals only with the mind. We are both mind and emotions. Spiritual experience demands a wholesome balance between the two. In spiritual experience, burning hearts can never be nourished by empty heads.

6. Spiritual formation is imperative in order to develop an inner support system which is adequate to master the difficult circumstances of one's life, such as stress, routine, failure, loss, overpowering workloads, and the unrealistic expectations of others. Inexplicable sufferings inevitably come to us. Life will overpower us, will destroy us unless we have adequate inward resources to match the pressures on the outside. Spiritual formation builds up the reservoir of inward spiritual energy, which makes possible masterful living.

7. Spiritual formation is imperative to enable a Christian to perform effectively the redemptive ministries assigned by Jesus Christ. The key to effectiveness is not personal ability or professional skills, but love.

8. Spiritual formation is imperative to insure our continuous replenishing as we engage in ministries to others. We dare not let our exports exceed our imports. We cannot give what we do not have. There is a rhythm to the spiritual life: life received, life poured out, life renewed, life poured out, and on and on.

9. Spiritual formation is imperative for the Christian to achieve a wholesome balance between the material and the spiritual. "The world is too much with us." We must have spiritual help to decide

    Who is master? The world or you?
    It is the eternal struggle;
    the world, so dramatic, so exciting;
    the Spirit, so gentle, so . . . still.

10. Spiritual formation is an imperative as an antidote to excessive individualism in spiritual experience. Spiritual formation is a communal as well as personal enterprise. We can never move forward in our spiritual experience alone. Our brothers and sisters must journey with us.

11. Spiritual formation is imperative to withstand the blights of institutionalism and rationalism. In the

presence of orthodox doctrine there is always the threat of rationalism—truth for its own sake, truth arrived at through its own methods, truth held onto by its own safeguards. Rationalism can be encountered only by a renewed sense of wonder in the experience of God's presence. Institutionalism is always a threat to the community of faith. It can be resisted only by making personal spiritual experience a priority within the boundaries of corporate love.

Spiritual formation has three essential characteristics. It must be intentional, structured, and disciplined.

Spiritual growth is never automatic; it just does not happen. It is always intentional. God takes the initiative. The Christian, inspired by the Holy Spirit, must accept the responsibility to respond and to participate in the process. This underscores the place of the will in spiritual experience. The Christian is emotional and rational but also volitional. The full weight of one's will must be placed on the side of one's participation in spiritual formation. Frank Laubach, emphasized "will-pressure," "will-bent," "will-act" as one's responsibility for spiritual growth.

Intention in the direction of spiritual formation grows out of intense spiritual desire. Frederick W. Faber said that "the lack of desire is the ill of all ills." A holy man once remarked, "At any given moment you are just as holy as you want to be." This calls for constant sensitivity, receptivity, and obedience and for keeping one's total self fully open and receptive to God's Spirit continually.

At one point in the play Hay Fever,[4] the leading actress says to a gentleman, "Come and lean attentively on the piano." The instructions were freighted with meaning: "Don't be just a casual observer of my piano playing; be attentive to my piano playing." Such spiritual attentiveness must characterize the Christian.

Second, spiritual formation also needs to be structured. Otherwise it is not carried on effectively. It cannot be pursued haphazardly. In one's adventure of growth the Christian must follow a working method by which he can live as a channel for the Holy Spirit. Such a plan must maintain a wholesome balance between devotion and action. It must be undergirded by sound biblical theology and be Christ-centered in its focus. It must also be personally congenial. It must be adjusted to one's present spiritual needs and be possible of fulfillment in view of one's daily circumstances. Not everybody is expected to pursue spiritual growth along the same avenues.

Some means by which a Christian may grow are:

1. BIBLE STUDY—for spiritual growth

2. THEOLOGICAL STUDY—gaining an understanding of the essentials of the Christian faith

3. DEVOTIONAL LITERATURE—a study of the writings of the spiritual leaders of the Christian centuries

4. PRAYER—learning how to pray effectively

5. SPIRITUAL DISCIPLINES—practicing disciplined living

6. COMMUNITY—learning that we need one another in the body of Christ

7. STEWARDSHIP—demonstrating the lordship of Jesus Christ over all aspects of one's life

8. WITNESSING AND EVANGELISM—personal obedience to Christ's Great Commission

9. SERVICE—manifesting the servant stance of Jesus Christ

10. PSYCHO-SOCIAL GROWTH—using the insights of psychology and sociology as a means to enhance the spiritual life

One cannot participate in all these areas at the same time. One must therefore set as priority his greatest spiritual need and for the time being focus upon the area that will be of the greatest help. When the results in a given area are positive, a person moves into another area, again according to personal need.

Third, spiritual formation must also be disciplined. Thomas Merton wrote, "It is not complicated to lead the spiritual life, but it is difficult"[5] *The Sign of Jonas*). When I use the term disciplined, I am not referring to the practice of personal disciplines which is a part of the structure of spiritual formation. Rather, I am thinking of the spirit and manner with which a person participates in the process of spiritual formation.

Disciplined means totality of dedication to growth, and the determination to avoid all hindrance.

Disciplined means regularity and continuity in one's devotion. John Wesley said that he intended to keep his prayer time early each morning "without exception." Oswald Chambers said it well: "You no more need a holiday from spiritual concentration than your heart needs a holiday from beating. You cannot have a moral holiday and remain moral, nor can you have a spiritual holiday and remain spiritual.[6]

Continuity and regularity are necessary in spite of one's feelings and moods. William James advised, "I think we ought to be independent of our moods, look on them as external (for they come to us unbidden), and feel if possible neither elated nor depressed, but keep our eyes upon our work." Dietrich Bonhoeffer in his writings on the Christian life, particularly in his volume *Life Together,* deals with the matter of moods and faith. He concludes emphatically that we must arrive at that state when our spirituality is never subject to our moods.

Disciplined means persistence. Spiritual growth is not achieved in ten easy lessons. It does not happen overnight nor does one of God's beautiful redwood trees grow overnight. Frank Laubach said, "It is a long process. Souls take longer than diamonds to form." Spiritual formation takes time. We must give the Holy Spirit time to move upon us and within us. We must "take time to be holy."

Spiritual formation is always a divine/human cooperative process. Paul says that since God is working in us we must work out our own salvation with fear and trembling (Phil. 2:12–13). The possibility of the spiritual life is the gift of the Spirit, but growth in the spiritual life is the responsibility of those who enter into it.

John Wesley wrote:

> Being born of God immediately and necessarily implies the continual inspiration of God's Holy Spirit—God breathing into the soul and the soul's breathing back what it first receives from God; a continued action of God upon the soul, and a reaction of the soul upon God; an unceasing presence of God, the loving, pardoning God, manifested to the heart, and perceived by faith; and an unceasing return of love, praise, and prayer, offering up all the thoughts of our hearts, all the words of our tongues, all the works of our hands, all our body, soul, and spirit, to be a holy sacrifice, acceptable unto God for Christ Jesus . . . God does not continue to act upon the soul, unless the soul reacts upon God . . . He will not continue to breathe unto our soul, unless our soul breathes toward him again.[7]

Gerald Heard, in his *Prayers and Meditations,* says that "grace is always sufficient, provided we are ready to cooperate with it."[8] After we receive the grace of God, its continuing effectiveness is the result of our devotion and discipline, inspired, and sustained by the Holy Spirit.

In commenting upon "My soul is even as a weaned child" (Ps. 131:2), Amy Carmichael says, "God did not mean us always to have the Living Water drawn for us and poured out into glasses and set on our tables. We are meant to DRAW WATER OUT OF THE WELL OF SALVATION ourselves" (Isa. 12:3).[9]

The Holy Spirit is the divine agent in the process of spiritual formation, but He never acts as an ends in Himself. He acts in order that "Christ may dwell in your hearts by faith, that being rooted and grounded in love, you may be able to comprehend . . . the love of God, that you may be filled with all the fullness of God" (Eph. 3:14–19).

What is the final outcome of our life-long participation in spiritual formation? "We shall be like him; for we shall see him as he is" (1 John 3:2). "And we, who with unveiled faces all reflect the Lord's glory, are being transformed into his likeness with ever-increasing glory, which comes from the Lord, who is the Spirit" (2 Cor. 3:18).

But in the meantime, under the inspiration of the Holy Spirit there are no limits to spiritual formation. Heraclitus wrote, "You cannot discover the boundaries of the soul by traveling in any direction."

THE HOLY SPIRIT EMPOWERS

Just before He ascended into heaven Jesus gave a final promise concerning the Holy Spirit: " . . . you shall receive power when the Holy Spirit has come upon you; and you shall be my witnesses in Jerusalem and in all Judea and Samaria and to the end of the earth" (Acts 1:8, RSV).

There are two dimensions to the Spirit-filled life: *being* and *doing*. Perhaps the three areas that we have already noted—enlightenment, enlivening, enrichment—have a primary reference to *being,* what a Christian is and is becoming. But the dimension of empowerment relates primarily to *doing*. The Holy Spirit comes to us not only to help us to be and to become, but also to help us do. He makes us the kind of persons we ought to be in order that we may do what Christ commands us to do. Frank Laubach remarked, "We can do no more than we are."

Even though being takes priority over doing, being is always in order to doing. Oswald Chambers wrote, "God is not after perfecting me to be a specimen in His show room; He is getting me to the place where He can use me. Let Him do what He likes."[10]

We need a correct understanding of the meaning of spiritual power. "To empower" means to enable, to qualify one. Power means adequacy to achieve an intended purpose. Power must be understood in degrees according to capacities and assignments. A few minutes ago I returned to my study after mowing my back lawn. I have a twenty-inch, self-propelling mower. The motor is small, but adequate. Never once did it even sputter while I was using it today. When that motor was designed for that mower the basic concern was adequacy.

I keep my lawn mower in my garage where my wife and I park our cars. Each automobile has a suitable engine, but I must confess that I have a preference for the power of one of them over the other, particularly when I am entering a double highway from our subdivision.

While I was mowing this afternoon I could hear planes taking off at the nearby airport. I knew that the motor which had been placed in each plane was considered adequate to lift that plane with its cargo of passengers and baggage off the runway smoothly and to guarantee its continuing flight to its destination.

I shall always remember the first time I flew on a 747. When I took my seat in the cabin, I looked around at the size of it and thought of the 350 passengers aboard, and all the stored cargo. I said to myself that it would never get off the ground. But then came the decisive moment of takeoff. What power, as that giant ship of the skies left the earth and slowly but surely attained a flying altitude. I thought also about the mighty engines in the *Queen Elizabeth* on which I crossed the Atlantic five times.

Many different motors—in a lawnmower, an automobile, a great ship, a plane. Try to imagine what would have happened if the wrong motors had been placed in the wrong machines!

Just so, spiritually, the power of the Holy Spirit means adequacy to perform the assignments given by Jesus Christ. We do not have the same assigned specific tasks, but we are to receive adequate power from the Holy Spirit to fulfill our particular tasks. God never intended that all Christians be the same and do the same and receive a fixed amount or a stereotyped quantity of spiritual power. The source of spiritual power is unlimited—individually adapted and to be personally appropriated.

Acts 1:8 declares plainly that the primary purpose of the gift of power from the Holy Spirit is for the purpose of witnessing to Jesus Christ. According to the Scriptures, we err when we seek spiritual power for any other primary purpose.

How, then, do we witness to Jesus Christ through the

power of the Holy Spirit? First of all, we witness through the authenticity of our personal experience with Christ. The high priest, religious rulers, and teachers of the law took knowledge of the early Christians that they had been with Jesus (Acts 4:13).

John Furz, in a letter to John Wesley, tells of a woman living ten miles from Manchester, England, who was hungry to know God. She borrowed shoes to walk to the city, hoping to find someone who could help her. She came to Manchester on a Sunday, but did not know where to go. Seeing a gentleman walking in the market place, she went to him and asked, "Where is it that people go to find the Lord?" He said, "Among the Methodists, as far as I know." And he led her to the Methodist preaching house where she found the Lord. What a graphic illustration of the power of personal experience to witness to Christ!

Christians also witness to Jesus through the Christlike quality of their lives. St. John of the Cross (1542–1591) compares humankind to a window through which the light of God is showing. If the window pane is clean of every stain, it is completely transparent, we do not see it all. It is "empty" and nothing is seen but the light. But if one bears in himself the stains of spiritual egotism and preoccupation with his illusory and exterior self, even in "good things," then the windowpane itself is clearly seen by reason of the stains that are on it.

Manifesting forgiveness is always a magnificent witness to Jesus Christ. Corrie ten Boom was such a witness in our own day. She was one of the few survivors of Ravensbruck, the concentration camp where 96,000 women died. In her book, *Tramp For the Lord,* she recounted her experience after she returned to Germany in 1947 to preach forgiveness. One night in a Munich church, she met one of her former guards. She was overwhelmed with memories of the man's inhuman cruelty. The guard approached Corrie, thrust out his hand and asked forgiveness. She stood frozen, unable to life her hand; her words about forgiveness echoed hollow in her ears.

Then . . . I prayed silently. "I can lift my hand. I can do that much." And so, woodenly, mechanically, I thrust my hand into the one stretched out to me. And as I did, . . . healing warmth seemed to flood my whole being, bringing tears to my eyes. "I forgive you, brother!", I cried. . . . For a long moment we grasped each other's hands, the former guard and the former prisoner. I had never known God's love so intensely as I did then."[11]

We usually think of witnessing as verbal. We speak a good word for Jesus Christ to someone who needs Him as Savior and Friend. We invite someone outside the kingdom of Christ to come in. As D. T. Niles remarked, we tell another beggar where to find bread. Such witnessing was the initial evidence of the power of the Holy Spirit on the first Christian Pentecost. The Spirit-filled disciples spoke about Christ in languages that were understood by the hearers (Acts 2:4–11). Throughout the book of the Acts are the records of faithful witnessing to Jesus Christ, as the Gospel was taken into all the then known world and people were born into the kingdom of Christ.

The history of the Christian centuries is the story of faithful witnessing to Christ. Every local church is the result of it. You and I are Christians because there were those who, having received the power of the Holy Spirit, were faithful in their witnessing.

So many Christians confess that they seem powerless when it comes to witnessing. This is not the norm for Christian living. The power of the Holy Spirit is given for just such witnessing. Jesus said, "Whoever acknowledges me before men, I will also acknowledge him before my Father in heaven. But whoever disowns me before men, I will disown him before my Father in heaven" (Matt. 10:32–33).

Evangelism is the corporate manifestation of personal witnessing. The church as a corporate society bears witness to the redeeming grace of Jesus Christ and calls sinners to repentance. And the effect is cumulative—individuals make it possible for the church to evangelize, and evangelizing churches take the Gospel into all the world. This was implied in the promise of the Holy Spirit's power: "You shall be my witnesses in Jerusalem and in all Judea and Samaria and to the end of the earth" (Acts 1:8, RSV).

We also bear witness to Christ through our compassion for the needy. God is spoken of as "the Father of compassion" (2 Cor. 1:3). Jesus was a person of great compassion. We are told that after a tour through the cities and villages of Galilee where He saw crowds with great personal needs, "he had compassion for them, because they were harassed and helpless, like sheep without a shepherd" (Matt. 9:35–36).

Compassion is more than mere pity. It means to suffer with another person in his or her needs. Such intensity of feeling for another in need results inevitably in activity to help such a person.

Such compassion becomes an authentic witness to Jesus Christ. Recall Toyohiko Kagawa, one of the great Christians of our century. He left his well-to-do circumstances in a comfortable location in Tokyo to move to Kobe and minister in an area known as the slums of Shinkawa. Throughout his life he concerned himself with the needy and the suffering, refusing any offer of positions of worldly influence. Such a life of compassion was in response to his prayer made early in his life: "O God, make me like Christ."

This was the spirit and ministry of Frank Laubach. He gave his life to the painstaking task of teaching people to read. I heard him say a number of times that at some point in that tedious and slow process someone being taught would ask, "Why are you doing this for me?" His answer was always the same: "Because Christ loves you and I love you."

Today Mother Teresa and her sisters move among the multitude of the poor, the outcast, the sick, the needy in the slums of Calcutta. Those who know the city speak of it as one of the neediest places in all the world. Why is she doing all this? Because of her love for the people, which was born of Christ's love for her and her love for Christ.

When she was leaving home in Yugoslavia to join the Irish order of the Sisters of Loreto in Dublin, her mother said to her, "You go, put your hand in Jesus' hand, and walk alone with Him." In 1968 she moved to the slums of Calcutta. Two years later she established the new religious order of the Missionaries of Charity which now numbers more than 1400 persons in sixty-seven countries of the world.

When asked what gives her and her sisters the strength to work in the streets of Calcutta from dawn to dusk, many times holding the nearly dead in their arms, she replied that it was not dedication to an abstract cause, but dedication to the person of a compassionate Christ. She has often said, "Spread love everywhere you go. To show love for God and our neighbor we need not do great things. It is how much love we put in the doing that makes our offering something beautiful for God."

In a volume now entitled *An Anthology of Devotional Literature* (originally *The Fellowship of the Saints*), Thomas Kepler has put together a compilation from the devotional writings of the centuries. He begins with Clement of Rome (first century A.D.) and continues through such twentieth-century greathearts as Stanley Jones, Frank Laubach, and Douglas Steere. So meaningful has this book been to me that I would classify it as indispensable in a Christian's library.

In his preface, Kepler gives ten characteristics of saints, truly a description of what happens when the Holy Spirit takes over.

1. A saint is a "religion-intoxicated" person.

2. A saint lives with a joyous, radiant, lighthearted freedom because his life is totally dependent on God.

3. A saint emulates Christ in everything he does.

4. A saint freely opens his life to God's agape—redemptive, free-giving love—and as the recipient of God's love he desires to help the needy, the lost, the unfortunate, the unhappy.

5. The saint looks upon Christianity not merely as a theoretical ideal; for him it is a practical way of living with individuals in an unchristian society.

6. A saint believes that the kingdom of God can come into history.

7. A saint has a continuous humility.

8. A saint looks wistfully into the eyes of every person, regardless of race, color, creed, or nation, as a brother or sister in whom lie the potentialities of a Christian saint.

9. A saint does not desire to escape the world through the act of devotion; rather he strives to use the results of worship to better the world.

10. A saint, like those pictured in beautiful cathedral windows, is a person through whom the light shines.[12]

4 | *TWO PRACTICAL MINISTRIES OF THE HOLY SPIRIT*

Those who are led by the Spirit of God are sons of God.

(Rom. 8:14)

He who raised Christ from the dead will also give life to your mortal bodies through his Spirit, who lives in you.

(Rom. 8:11)

Two ministries of the Holy Spirit are of extremely practical importance to contemporary Christians: guidance and healing.

GUIDANCE

There is much confusion about guidance in Christian circles. How often we hear someone say, "The Spirit told me to do it," or "the Spirit made me do it," or "the Spirit directed me to say it." The problem arises when what is said or done is not within the parameters of the biblical revelation or of Christlikeness, on the one hand; or when the course of speaking or acting, which is professed to be Spirit-led, does not work out as intended.

Some so-called "Spirit guidance" has turned out to be disastrous in its consequences. In some the results of following what was believed to be divine guidance were so opposite to what was intended, that there followed either an attitude of murmuring against the Lord or a noticeable casualty in faith. Is it not logical to suppose that if God told a

73

person to do something, it would turn out right? But when such ventures fail, is it justifiable to blame God, who is supposed to have directed from the beginning? A seminarian once said to me, "We need to get our heads screwed on straight in reference to such a practical matter as being divinely guided."

Let us begin by confessing our need of divine guidance. Oswald Chambers prayed, "Lord, Thy ways are like Thyself—perfect; my ways are like myself—imperfect. Touch me into effectual identity with Thy consciousness, and with Thy ways for this day." Frank Laubach once remarked, "You will worry less when you learn better what guidance means."

Divine guidance is promised the Christian:

He guides me in the right paths, as he has promised (Ps. 23:3, TEV).

He leads the humble in the right way and teaches them his will (Ps. 25:9, TEV).

The LORD says, I will teach you the way you should go; I will instruct you and advise you (Ps. 32:8, TEV).

The LORD guides a man in the way he should go and protests those who please him (Ps. 37:23, TEV).

This God is our God forever and ever; he will lead us for all time to come (Ps. 48:14, TEV).

You guide me with your instruction (Ps. 73:24, TEV).

Remember the LORD in everything you do, and he will show you the right way" (Prov. 3:6, TEV).

I will always guide you (Isa. 58:11, TEV).

If you wander off the road to the right or the left, you will hear his voice behind you, saying, "Here is the road. Follow it" (Isa. 30:21, TEV).

Jesus declared, "I am the way" (John 14:6); "I am the light of the world; whoever follows me will have the light of life and will never walk in darkness" (John 8:12, TEV); "When the Spirit of truth comes . . . he will lead you into all the truth" (John 16:13, TEV).

The Apostle Paul wrote, "Those who are led by God's

Spirit are God's sons" (Rom. 8:14, TEV); "Don't be fools, then, but try to find out what the LORD wants you to do" (Eph. 5:17, TEV).

The Apostle James assures us, "If any of you lacks wisdom, let him ask of God who gives to all men generously and without reproaching, and it will be given him" (1:5).

The Scriptures are replete with illustrations of divine guidance. Abraham's servant said that the Lord led him "straight to my master's relatives" (Gen. 24:27, TEV). Joseph's response to the evil deeds of his brothers against him implied divine guidance in his life: "You plotted evil against me, but God turned it into good" (Gen. 50:20, TEV). God guided the Israelites through the wilderness by a pillar of cloud by day and a pillar of fire by night (Ex. 13:21–22).

Paul believed himself divinely guided both personally and vocationally. During his missionary journeys, he made particular reference to the time when he was forbidden to preach the Word in the province of Asia, and the door opened to enter Europe with the Gospel (Acts 16:6–7).

There is a beautiful reference to corporate guidance in the divine message to the church at Philadelphia, recorded in Revelation 3:7: "When he opens a door, no one can close it, and when he closes it, no one can open it."

Is divine guidance for everyone, irrespective of one's spiritual sensitivities or relationships? Any satisfying answer to this question must come from Scripture. Paul says that "the sons of God" are the ones led by the Spirit of God (Rom. 8:14). "The sons of God" are those who have received the witness of the Spirit (vv. 15–16) and have experienced self-crucifixion through Him (v. 13).

In Psalm 23 guidance is promised to those who have made God their Good Shepherd. In Psalm 25:9 humility is singled out as an essential for guidance. Other times the psalmist says that guidance is for the one who has made the Lord his hiding place (32:7), and for the one who has made a permanent covenant with God (48:14). In Proverbs 3:5–7 we are told that guidance is for the one who makes a continual acknowledgment of God in all the affairs of his life.

The prophets reserve guidance for God's chosen people

(Isa. 30:21; 58:11), and for those who seek it, wait for it, and are willing to obey it when it comes (Jer. 42:3).

It appears that divine guidance is the privilege of those who sustain a close relationship to God and who seek to be sensitive to His will at all times. It is not the prerogative merely of God's special ones, chosen for selective ministries, but it is for all those who seek to walk humbly with their God. This does not exclude a form of divine guidance which relates to all God's creatures through His general providence, but the concept of "being divinely guided" seems to have a particular reference to God's children, to those who have entered into a personal relationship with Him through Christ.

How extensive is God's guidance? Does God guide individuals directly as well as through the group? Does guidance extend beyond religious matters into secular affairs? Is God interested in the minor as well as the major decisions of life?

Certainly, divine guidance includes direct personal guidance as well as guidance through the group. If divine guidance does not extend beyond strictly religious matters into the affairs of everyday life, of what real value is the Spirit-filled experience, since Christians spend most of their time in the workaday world? If we believe in the "control of the Spirit," is there not the constant guidance of the Holy Spirit even when we may not be consciously seeking it?

No decision of a Christian's life is incidental or meaningless. After all, life is made up largely of a series of little decisions. The manner of discovering divine guidance in major, momentous decisions may be different from that in seeking continuing guidance in all the affairs of life, but it must be affirmed that the steps of a good person—all the steps, little steps, big steps—are ordered by the Lord.

How does God guide the Spirit-filled person? George Müller, that great man of faith, said in this regard:

1. I seek at the beginning to get my heart into such a state that it has no will of its own in regard to a given matter. Nine-tenths of the trouble with people

is just here. Nine-tenths of the difficulties are overcome when our hearts are ready to do the Lord's will, whatever it may be. When one is truly in this state, it is usually but a little way to the knowledge of what His will is.

2. Having done this, I do not leave the result to feeling of a simple impression.

3. I seek the will of the Spirit of God through, or in connection with, the Word of God. The Spirit and the Word must be combined. If I look to the Spirit alone without the Word, I lay myself open to great delusions also. If the Holy Ghost guides us at all, He will do it according to the Scriptures and never contrary to them.

4. Next, I take into account providential circumstances. These often indicate God's will in connection with His Word and Spirit.

5. I ask God in prayer to reveal His will to me aright.

6. Thus, through prayer to God, the study of the Word, and reflection, I come to a deliberate judgment according to the best of my ability and knowledge, and if my mind is thus at peace and continues so after two or three more petitions, I proceed accordingly.

F. B. Meyer, well-known devotional writer, gives an interesting illustration of divine guidance:

When I was crossing the Irish Channel one dark, starless night, I stood on the deck by the captain and asked him, "How do you know Holy Head Harbor on so dark a night as this?" He said, "You see those three lights? Those three must line up behind each other as one, and when we see them so united we know the exact position of the Harbor's mouth."

When we want to know God's will there are three things which always concur—the inward impulse, the Word of God, and the trend of circumstances. God in the heart impelling you forward; God in His book corroborating whatever He says in the heart; God in circumstances which are always indicative of His will. Never start until these three things agree.

In his book *How Does God Guide Us?*, E. Stanley Jones presents eight ways through which he believes the Spirit-filled Christian receives God's guidance:

1. Through the life and teaching of Jesus as contained in the Scriptures

2. Through the accumulated wisdom of the centuries, mediated to us through the church

3. Through disciplined group guidance

4. Through individual counsel

5. Through opening providences

6. Through the discovery of natural law by scientific investigation

7. Through our heightened moral intelligence

8. Through the Inner Voice

Divine guidance is a cooperative enterprise. While God is always taking the initiative and offering His gifts, it is the Christian's responsibility to respond accordingly and to cooperate fully.

Consider specific steps in receiving divine guidance. To begin with, the Christian must recognize the difference between merely human tendencies and divine influences. There is a difference between humanity per se and the human when it is influenced by the divine. We must learn to distinguish between compulsions, impressions, and inspirations. Compulsions are basically human, including both natural and acquired prejudices. Impressions are personal reactions to both inward and external stimuli. Inspirations come from the Holy Spirit. The bottom line is that compulsions and impressions may not necessarily be avenues of divine guidance. On the other hand, inspirations of the Spirit always are.

Thomas C. Upham included in his book *Inward Divine*

Guidance a section on "how to discern between impulses and a sanctified judgment."

> Sometimes persons act from certain interior impressions termed *impulses*. It would be very injurious to the cause of holiness if mere interior impressions became the rule of conduct to a holy person.

> Sometimes men have mistaken natural impulses for the secret inspirations of the Spirit and, in the flattering belief of being guided by a higher power, have experienced no other guidance than their own rebellious passions. On the danger of such a state, of which the church has seen too many melancholy instances, it is unnecessary to remark.[1]

Second, the guidance of the Holy Spirit is always within the parameters of the revelations of Scripture. Spiritually-minded persons covet a religious experience in depth, in which divine guidance is personal and sure. But such spiritual desires must not lead to unwarranted off-limits or to peripheral tangents. God's voice of revelation never opposes the recorded ordinances of God in the Holy Scriptures.

In one of my early churches I was told of a person in the community who had once announced that God promised him that he would be protected if he jumped from the roof of a large barn. He announced a date and time for the fulfillment of the supposed miracle. A crowd assembled. The man went to the peak of the roof. While the crowd waited breathlessly, the man suddenly began climbing down from the barn. When he reached the ground he announced that God had given him a further revelation—not to jump.

There is nothing in the Scriptures which authorizes divine protection for such foolish acts. Even Jesus, the Son of God, refused to jump from the pinnacle of the temple, presuming that God's angels would protect Him.

Third, the content of divine guidance is always within the bounds of Christlikeness. The Spirit is "another" Comforter. Who is the "first" Comforter? Jesus Christ. The quality of the Spirit's ministrations is always Christlike. The

Spirit will never tell a person to say or do a thing, or react in a manner which is not Christlike. I recall a self-assured minister who once challenged my spirituality because I belonged to a mainline denomination. In response to some derogatory remarks he made about my spiritual convictions, I commented "You insult me with talk like that." He retorted immediately, "If I insult you, then God called me to insult you." Such an attitude misses the meaning of God's call and the Spirit's guidance.

Fourth, the guidance of the Holy Spirit is never contrary to Spirit-enlightened intelligence. Reason was one of John Wesley's doctrinal guidelines, the others being Scripture, tradition, and experience.

Fifth, discernment is usually a factor in guidance. Discernment is the ability to identify reality in spiritual matters, to know when Christ is speaking. The apostle John writes that we are not to believe every spirit, but to test the spirits to see whether they are of God (1 John 4:1–3). The apostle says that the world is filled with spirits and many of these spirits are incarnated in persons. But some of the spirits are "antichrist" instead of "Christ-spirits," and we must make a careful distinction between the two. John identifies the spirit sent from God: It is the spirit that confesses that Jesus Christ is come in the flesh. Thus, Jesus Christ is the content, the spirit, and the purpose of divine revelation.

Sixth, usually, except in crisis situations, the indications of divine guidance are both progressive and persistent. As the indications continue to appear, they are consistent rather than contradictory. But more than this, there is a spiritual pressure upon the consciousness as to the rightness of the core of the indications. Isaiah described such a pressure: "The Lord spoke thus to me with his strong hand upon me, and warned me" (Isa. 8:11, RSV).

Seventh, at some point in the seeking of divine guidance, insights and help should be solicited from trusted Christians. Seeking group guidance should not be an initial activity. However, there comes a time when indications of guidance should be tested by the response of a disciplined group.

Group guidance is much more specific than general church guidance. Where a group is closely knit and disciplined there can be a surrender of the group will to God, a letting down of barriers, a passive relaxation in the Presence, an alert listening. God will guide that group. Under the inspiration of the Holy Spirit a common mind will emerge.

It was said of the group at Antioch that as they fasted and prayed, the Holy Spirit said, "Set apart for me Barnabas and Saul for the work to which I have called them" (Acts 13:2). The group received guidance for the individuals within the group. One of the most beautiful statements in the Scriptures is the statement of the early church in relation to a particular crisis: "It seemed good to the Holy Spirit and to us" (Acts 15:28). Their minds and His were in tune, and the message could get across.

Eighth, guidance is to be followed as it is revealed, even if revealed in piecemeal fashion. Frank Laubach has said, "The way is discovered by following it, by walking through open doors. Work at the thing or person near you until I show you where else you are needed, and then follow guidance there. Never refuse; never hesitate."

Ninth, faith helps us to become sensitive to the divine timing in the process of guidance. Paul Tournier writes, "Living in the plan of God isn't just a matter of doing what God wants, but of doing it *when* he wants."[2]

John Henry Jowett told of an experience in which he became panicky at the beginning of a week during which he had to make a crucial decision. He was becoming impatient because he did not seem to be receiving the guidance which he sought from God. As he discussed the matter with his wife, she asked him, "And when must you make this decision?" He replied, "On Friday." Then calmly but decisively his wife responded, "But this is only Tuesday."

Tenth, the most crucial step in the process of divine guidance is the actual moment when the guidance is obeyed. It is always a step of faith. Robert Raines writes:

> Biblical faith is not knowledge. It is not having answers, but being driven and drawn by questions. Faith is not

managing our destiny, but losing control of our destiny. Faith requires us to learn to trust the process. Faith is the pursuit of understanding—and no longer of certainty. Faith is commitment without all the evidence being in. Faith is learning to trust God in the dark. Faith is risk as well as promise, and darkness in the tunnel as well as the hope of light at the end of the tunnel.

Thomas Merton stated it beautifully: "My Lord God, I have no idea where I am going. I do not see the road ahead of me. I cannot know for certain where it will end . . . I believe that the desire to please you does in fact please you . . . and I know that if I do this you will lead me by the right road."[3]

Oswald Chambers also witnesses to such a step of faith.

My mind is still vague regarding the way I am to take, Lord; so much has gone beyond my own discernment in this decision. It is not that I doubt Thee, but all is so completely shrouded.

Lord, a vague desolation seems around my life, it is nebulous, I cannot define it. I have no misgiving over my decision for I have done what Thou didst indicate I should do, but still the sense of uncertainty remains. Touch this nebulous nimbus and turn it into a firmament of ordered beauty and form.

Few have understood better the nature and process of divine guidance than Frank Laubach, who wrote in his devotional notes:

How can we find Thy will, God?

Simply say at any moment, Thy will be done; then do what you believe is your part and watch the results. Thus, you will see what I desire in any situation.

Life will be a succession of ventures of faith, not trying to be sagacious but only crammed with love. Like manna from heaven, my guidance must be fresh each morning and each minute.

Perhaps the validity of divine guidance may be actually discovered in that initial moment of personal decision to obey. My wife gave me an insight into this matter. She has observed that once a Spirit-filled Christian accepts the divine invitation, the fulfillment of the guidance is assured. If this is true, then a person does not have to seek continuing confirmation of having made the right decision, but rather has only to implement it. Sooner or later the "rightness" of guidance will be confirmed. "He guides me in the right paths" (Ps. 23:3, TEV). There is no set pattern for such authentication nor is there any uniform schedule that applies to all Christians. Sometimes it is the confirmation of fruitful ministry. Other times it is the opening and closing doors in one's circumstances. Often it is the witness of one's inner consciousness, the personal sense deep within that through unfolding guidance one is experiencing fulfillment, the abundant life.

The apostle Paul was confident that ultimately he would lay hold of the reason why the hand of God reached down and laid hold of him on the Damascus Road (Phil. 3:12). Years after the miraculous saving of his life in the fire at the Epworth Rectory, John Wesley declared, "I am a brand plucked from the burning." Wilfred Grenfell, missionary to Labrador, said that he was as sure of the hand of God on his life as he was of the hand of the pilot on the wheel of his boat, as he traveled along the coast and in and out of the harbors. E. Stanley Jones told how the Inner Voice called him from his prayer time, which he tried to keep inviolate, to the deck of the ship. There he discovered that his baggage, intended for India, was mistakenly being put off at Southhampton. He testified, "I am confident that God will take care even of the baggage."

Norman Vincent Peale was once led to take a particular train from New York to Chicago, and at breakfast to go to the dining car at a particular time and sit at a table with another traveler. During that meal Dr. Peale received from his new-found friend invaluable insights and counsel which led to the making of a crucial decision in his life. Peale said, "If you will let God guide you, you will get on the right train, go to the dining car at the right time, and sit at the right table." A retiring bishop once commented: "My entire life has been a personally conducted tour by the Eternal."

During my years at Asbury Theological Seminary, many students told me of divine guidance in their lives. Sometimes the guidance related to an initial decision to enter the ministry or to change vocations. Some were led in unusual ways in a particular choice of schooling.

All of these testimonies are fascinating and deeply moving. They all point to the reality of divine guidance and to a personal consciousness that it was actually happening. A final comment: Naturally the Christian's ability to experience continuing guidance grows by what one has already experienced of it. We learn by experience.

Frank Laubach records a conversation God had with him:

> You will be educated in My will by experiments through each day; the more constantly you make these experiments the wider will be your cumulative knowledge of My will.
>
> Tingling with the glory of God's moment-by-moment leadership, feeling new power surging through [our] veins, new vision filling our minds, we know we are on a new trail and that it has limitless possibilities. Because it is new, we do not know where it is going. We are on our toes with eager expectancy, sure that He who holds all the secrets of endless ages in His hand, who knows more than all the Houdinis or Einsteins together, not only can and will but also longs to give His unimaginable plenty to those who listen.

How thrilling is the realization that guidance is always latent with God's serendipities!

SPIRITUAL HEALING

Paul writes, "He who raised Christ from the dead will also give life to your mortal bodies through his Spirit, who lives in you" (Rom. 8:11). Most commentators agree that this verse has reference to our mortal bodies before they are made immortal. It is a reference to the healing power of the Holy Spirit in our present condition. E. Stanley Jones made this verse the basis of his belief in day-by-day healing through the power of the Holy Spirit who is the quickener of life and the divine agent in healing.

What is spiritual healing? It is the process of the restoration of wholeness to a person in any area of need, or in totality. It relates to the healing of the mind, the emotions, the spirit, the body, and also relationships, which are an added dimension of human personality.

Jesus performed His healing ministry in the power of the Holy Spirit. In the Gospels are records of at least twenty-six healing miracles that Jesus performed upon individuals. There are numerous other references to multiple healings. A medical classification shows that Jesus healed the following known ailments: fever, malaria, leprosy, congenital blindness, Parkinson's disease, nephritis, arthritis, fibroids of the uterus or functional hemorrhage, epilepsy, deafness, crippledness, and insanity. And certainly Jesus must have also encountered the neurotic conditions that are associated with these, such as fear, anxiety, insomnia, nervousness, palpitation, heart disorder, indigestion, excitement, and depression.

When Jesus sent forth His disciples He instructed them, among other things, to heal the sick. "He called his twelve disciples to him and gave them authority to drive out evil spirits and to heal every disease and sickness" (Matt. 10:1).

Note that healing is a part of Jesus' Great Commission: "Go preach—go teach—go heal." William Barclay writes, "Preaching, teaching, healing—that was the three-fold pattern of the ministry of Jesus. Healing was an inseparable part of the work and the pattern of His apostles."

Healing was a regular ministry in the early church. It was the continuation of Jesus' healing works. The apostles healed in the name and power of Jesus, the divine Son of God (Acts 3:6, 16; 19:11–13). This was a dramatic evidence of the aliveness of Jesus Christ. He was in their very midst, performing His mighty works. Paul declared that the gift of healing is one of the gifts of the Holy Spirit (1 Cor. 12:9).

Has this spiritual gift of healing, so prominent in the early church, ever been withdrawn? Some may say that it has, but no internal or external evidence supports the claim. Rather, it appears that the gift of healing remains the possession of the church as the whole body of believers. In New Testament times the gift of healing was given for the common good. Thus it is logical to believe that the gift of healing now belongs to the contemporary church in the same way, under divine inspiration.

So today the church is intended to have a healing ministry through the power of the Spirit. Never has there been a time when so many people needed wholeness and healing. Not only is the church able to release faith which is essential in all healing, but the church should specialize in helping people experience positive emotions, which are the secret of the cure of psychosomatic illnesses.

Healing is related to faith in five ways.

1. To begin with, the Christian faith inspires healthful living, and this is the best prevention of disease. Medical specialists have often observed that if a person would start living the Christian way early enough in life, most sicknesses would never occur.

2. The Christian faith is also able to aid healing through scientific methods by the creation of the proper attitudes within the patient. All healing requires the will to live. Faith is the greatest inspirer and sustainer of such a positive stance.

3. At times the church's ministry of healing and medical science have joined hands to effect a healing, each contributing something to the healing that the other could not. Often neither spiritual healing alone nor mere scientific methods of healing alone are adequate. Both are needed; they become complementary to each other. With increasing recognition of this truth the greatest strides in the healing ministry of the church will be made in the future.

4. Next, the Christian faith is able to direct the healing of all those functional illnesses that have been

specifically caused by wrong mental, emotional, or spiritual attitudes.

There is a difference between an organic or structural illness and a functional or psychosomatic illness. A functional illness is one in which nothing is inherently wrong with an organ of the body, but an organ is malfunctioning. What is the cause? The answer is clear: wrong mental attitudes or negative emotions or improper spiritual relationships or a combination of these. Doctors estimate conservatively that eighty percent of all sickness is functional or psychosomatic in nature.

How devastating is the effect of wrong mental attitudes, negative emotions, and improper spiritual relationships! Every negative emotion, except the normal expression of grief, is destructive. Such things as fear, anxiety, ill will, guilt, inferiority, and negativism are destructive in their effect upon the human personality and can cause illness.

The only effective way to deal with functional illnesses is to deal with their basic causes. The mind must be disciplined away from wrong mental attitudes and into the direction of positive and constructive thinking. The heart must be filled with new spiritual energies. Negative emotions must be replaced by positive emotions. The guilt-ridden must find true forgiveness. Fear must be replaced by faith, anxiety by confidence. Ill will and resentments must give way to genuine love. A sense of hostility must be replaced by an attitude of acceptance in Christ. Inferiority attitudes must be supplanted by a sense of adequacy through spiritual resources. Negativism must be rejected as an antichristian attitude. A sense of futility must be replaced by a sense of divine purpose for one's life. All relationships must be reconciled in conformity with the teachings and example of Jesus Christ. All of this is possible only through the power of Jesus Christ actively at work within a spiritually responsive and fully cooperative person.

5. Finally, there is healing by the direct activity of God apart from the use of intermediary physical or psychological methods. This is God intervening directly in a person's experience, apart from all recognizable human sources of remedy, bringing healing that is clearly demonstrable. Human experience offers irrefutable evidence of the healing power of God after human skill has proved ineffective.

The Holy Spirit guides in the process of healing. It seems evident that there are six clear steps, through which a person passes in pursuit of healing. The Holy Spirit actively guides in each of them.

Relaxation

"Be still, and know that I am God" (Ps. 46:10). The body must be relaxed and freed of all tension. In fact, the body must be forgotten so that the mind can concentrate on God and on His healing power. The mind must also be relaxed. The presence of God cannot be realized by a restless spirit.

Purging

"If we walk in the light, as he is in the light, we have fellowship with one another, and the blood of Jesus, his Son, purifies us from all sin" (1 John 1:7). The subconscious mind must be cleansed of all wrong emotions and sinful states so that the healing power of God can flow through it. There must be the consciousness of divine forgiveness in the soul. God's healing power can work only in those who are living in accord with his laws.

Clarification

Jesus asked two blind men, "What do you want me to do for you?" (Matt. 20:32) A person must be specific, not general, in his request for healing. He must visualize exactly his need and vocalize his desire.

Consecration

"Whether we live or die, we belong to the Lord" (Rom. 14:8). One of the conditions of divine healing is this spiritual attitude of the absolute surrender of life to the will of God.

If the will of God be that health is restored immediately, then let God be praised. If health cannot be restored at once, then let the seeker realize that God is in every human circumstance and that ultimately His purpose will be made manifest. The seeker must be characterized by a sincere willingness to glorify God and to live for others. Healing, when received, cannot be hoarded selfishly. The renewed strength and the restored health are to be dedicated to God for the blessing and the service of others.

Anticipation

This is the step of faith. "Faith is being sure of what we hope for, and certain of what we do not see" (Heb. 11:1). There must be an eager expectancy, an active faith. Never must a seeker think in terms of failure. Always there is the anticipation of God fulfilling what He has already promised. One needs to visualize himself as healed.

Faith for healing involves the use of the imagination. Like every other faculty, the Christian's imagination should be sanctified. Such a sanctified imagination in its relation to healing demands that one should sustain in imagination only pictures of God at work in his body: annihilating germs, subduing toxins, repairing diseased tissues. Lightfoot's translation of Hebrews 11:1 suggests that "faith is that which gives reality to things hoped for."

One of the chief obstacles in healing is the old mindset, the preoccupation with disease or some habitual notion about its incurability, or some stubbornness of opinion which, once having denied the possibility of spiritual healing, is reluctant to admit its error. God is hampered in His desire to heal by negatives of intellectual doubt and imaginations.

Thus, in seeking healing, there must be the spirit of anticipation.

Appropriation

"I can do everything through him who gives me strength" (Phil. 4:13). The seeker receives what God has promised, begins acting in the strength of the healing power received, and is grateful to God for the reality. "Father, I thank you," is the personal appropriation of the divine blessings.

Let me suggest something which evangelicals have often seemed to overlook. Participation in Holy Communion is participation in the healing power of the Spirit. When rightly understood, Holy Communion is a healing sacrament as well as a convicting, regenerating, and sanctifying sacrament.

In this regard I think often of these words of Jesus: "Truly, truly, I say to you, unless you eat the flesh of the Son of man and drink his blood, you have no life in you; he who eats my flesh and drinks my blood has eternal life, and I will raise him up at the last day. For my flesh is food indeed, and my blood is drink indeed" (John 6:53–56, RSV).

Many of us believe that when we partake of the bread and the wine of Holy Communion, mystically we are eating Christ's body and drinking His blood. If so, then in fulfillment of His promise we receive His life into our own lives. His life is truly healing life and as it flows through every part of our being we partake of its healing power. As Charles Wesley sang in "O for a Thousand Tongues to Sing," "'Tis life, and health, and peace."

The life-giving power of the Holy Spirit anoints the inner man, which in turn transforms it into the *vis medicatrix naturae,* the healing force of nature that restores and renews the physical body. Were we humans fully alive to the creative potentialities of the Holy Spirit, we would not only attain personal health, but also bring healing to the rest of the world's creatures.

Healing comes through prayer. All true prayer is inspired by the Holy Spirit. As Dame Julian of Norwich taught, it is God the Holy Spirit who is the foundation of our praying, the ground of our beseeching.

Not only does the Holy Spirit manifest His healing power within individuals, but He also exhorts the church to become God's healing community. When the church responds positively to the Spirit's entreaties, it can become Gods great healing channel. To that end the church can

1. Teach and preach the gospel of health and healing

2. Cooperate with all other legitimate agencies of healing in the community

3. Be a support group for the sick
   a. those recovering
   b. those who will not recover

4. Provide worship and fellowship opportunities that are genuinely therapeutic in their effects

5. Maintain a vital revival and evangelism program. The deepest of all healing is that of the soul in its relationship to God and to others. Such spiritual healing often results in healing in other areas of the person's life.

6. Utilize the healing power of the sacraments

7. Sponsor active prayer groups that exercise continuing intercessory ministry for healing

8. Conduct regular healing services

9. Provide opportunities for healing counseling
   a. pre-crisis counseling
   b. ministry during crises

10. Carry on a ministry of reconciliation between alienated person and groups

11. Be concerned about societal healing

12. Train its members to be ministers of healing
    a. in personal, family, and social relationships
    b. in vocational opportunities—teachers, doctors, lawyers, nurses, executives

5 | THE HOLY SPIRIT AND THE CHURCH

> You are . . . fellow citizens with God's people and members of God's household, built on the foundation of the apostles and prophets, with Jesus Christ himself as the chief cornerstone. In him the whole building is joined together and rises to become a holy temple in the Lord. And in him you too are being built together to become a dwelling in which God lives by his Spirit.
>
> *(Eph. 2:19–22)*

On the day of Pentecost the Holy Spirit was given to the church and for the church. If it is true that "without the Holy Spirit, no church," it is just as true that "without the church, no Pentecost-gift of the Holy Spirit in His fullness." Even though the church was instituted by Jesus Christ at Caesarea Philippi (Matt. 16:13–19), it was constituted on Pentecost (Acts 2) and the Spirit was given to consolidate and undergird such ecclesiastical constitution.

The baptismal formula of St. Hippolytus (perhaps as early as the late second century) contains the question: "Do you believe in the Holy Spirit in the holy church?" The Apostles' Creed, which undoubtedly is indebted to the formula of Hippolytus, associates the Holy Spirit with the church: "I believe in the Holy Spirit, the holy catholic church, the communion of saints. . . ."

It is a gross misconception to make the gift of the Holy Spirit solely a matter of individual possession. He is also a corporate possession. This is illustrated symbolically in two

93

of the physical phenomena on the first day of Pentecost. There was the sound as of a rushing mighty wind which filled all the house where the early Christians were waiting. This signified the coming of the Spirit to the group as a group. But a tongue of fire was also distributed to each Christian, symbolizing the Spirit's gift of Himself to individuals.

The church is more than a group of people who have received the Holy Spirit individually. The church is a corporate body into which we are grafted by the Spirit. Origen wrote, "We are most of all God's temple when we prepare ourselves to receive the Holy Spirit." Pentecost should be viewed as the decisive introduction of the Christian church into the fulfillment of the redemptive purposes of God. F. W. Dillistone writes:

> The SPIRIT is pre-eminently the title applied to God in action.
>
> Under the pre-Christian order, the Spirit came upon chosen men, inspiring them and constraining them to share in the divine activity in word and deed.
>
> The Messiah of God was endued with the Spirit (without measure) and went about performing deeds of mercy and speaking words of salvation in accordance with the mission to which God had called Him.
>
> After His death and resurrection He poured out His Spirit upon His expectant followers, constituting them thereby His own body, His church, and bestowing upon them all the resources that they needed for their work and witness and community life. In this way there came into being THE SPIRIT-FILLED COMMUNITY.[1]

Consider now what the Holy Spirit already has done for the church. The Holy Spirit prepared for the church during Old Testament times. At the heart of the Old Testament concept of "the people of God," "the remnant of God" is the foreshadowing of the church of the new dispensation. God's chosen ones were ultimately to be bound more closely to Him through the church. The holy hill of Zion was but a foreglimpse of the Holy City. Jerusalem, the center of nationalistic hopes throughout the history of the Old Testament, was to be superseded by the New Jerusalem, universal, all-inclusive, spiritually-oriented. God's house was to become a house of prayer for all people. The Gospel was to be taken to all nations, and from the North and South and from the East and West would develop a community of faith and witness. As we read the Old Testament, we sense God's plan for the church yet to come. As we read the New Testament, we are confident that the hopes of the Old Dispensation are now fulfilled in the living church of Jesus Christ.

The Holy Spirit also prepared for the coming of the New Testament church by His inspired predictions regarding Messiah's coming and by His anointing of the Messiah. Jesus acknowledged this relationship when He established the church in His inaugural sermon in the synagogue in His home town of Nazareth: "The Spirit of the Lord is on me, because he has anointed me to preach good news to the poor. He has sent me to proclaim freedom for the prisoners and recovery of sight for the blind, to release the oppressed, to proclaim the year of the Lord's favor" (Luke 4:18–19).

The anointed Messiah at the close of His earthly ministry offered the gift of the Holy Spirit to those who were to be responsible for His church. But the Holy Spirit actually constituted the church on the day of Pentecost. The Spirit fell, and within a matter of a few hours three thousand persons were converted to the Christian faith. Through the Spirit the church at last became visible to the world. The book of Acts gives evidence of how quickly a hostile world recognized the presence of a new spiritual community.

The Spirit gave the church a clear perspective of its redemptive message and mission. The message is this: Jesus Christ died for our sins; He is risen from the dead; He is alive forevermore. The mission is this: "Therefore go and make disciples of all nations, baptizing them in the name of the Father and of the Son and of the Holy Spirit, and teaching them to obey everything I have commanded you" (Matt. 28:19–20), " . . . that repentance and forgiveness of sins should be preached in his name to all nations, beginning from Jerusalem" (Luke 24:47, RSV).

The Holy Spirit was also active in the consolidation of the church through the evolution of the organized structure of the church. At first the government of the church was simple, with the apostles naturally assuming the role of leadership. Then the diaconate developed when the need for caring for the poor arose. Eventually the structure of the church became much more elaborate, with institutionalized developments occurring in local churches and with local churches becoming related to one another in various hierarchical forms.

It is not to be understood that the Holy Spirit is personally responsible for every aspect of ecclesiastical organization. The chaff and the wheat, the good and the bad, the wise and the unwise will have to be sifted in the light of usefulness and spiritual effectiveness. But it is inevitable that spiritual ideals, to become effective, must be institutionally embodied in some manner and the Holy Spirit has always been at work in such a necessary process.

The Holy Spirit has also been the secret of power for the church as a corporate body. The Spirit always empowers the church to fulfill its redemptive ministries of worship, preaching, teaching, fellowship, service, and healing. He manifests His power in the church by means of the "gifts of the Spirit." We need to distinguish the gift of the Spirit from the gifts of the Spirit, and both from the fruit of the Spirit. The gift of the Spirit is God's offer of the fullness of Spirit to every Christian believer. Pentecost has been repeated every time a believer down through the centuries has received the Spirit in His fullness.

The fruit of the Spirit refers to the kind of spiritual character that the Holy Spirit produces in a person who has received the gift of the Spirit. Paul identifies nine aspects of the fruit: love, joy, peace, patience, kindness, goodness, faithfulness, gentleness, and self-control (Gal. 5:22–23).

The gifts of the Spirit are distinct from both the gift and the fruit of the Spirit. Spiritual gifts are a phenomenon of the dispensation of the Holy Spirit. They are extraordinary powers given for the purpose of serving the church in specific ministries. We can identify at least five characteristics of spiritual gifts:

1. They are charismatic in nature; that is, they are the gifts of God's grace, totally unmerited from any human viewpoint. The Greek word for "gift" is *charisma,* a distinctly New Testament word referring to God's favor, a gift of divine grace. The plural, *charismata,* in Pauline usage refers to a variety of enablings by the Holy Spirit so that selected individuals could serve the church in particular ways. But every manifestation of the *charismata* focuses upon the operation of divine grace, never upon mere human ability.

2. Spiritual gifts have a common source—the Holy Spirit.

3. There is a variety of spiritual gifts. According to Paul in 1 Corinthians 12, we need to distinguish among "gifts" (v. 4), "administrations" (v. 5), and "operations" (v. 6).

   Nine distinct spiritual gifts are spoken of in 1 Corinthians 12:8–10). Three of the gifts are "revelation" gifts: the *word of wisdom,* the *word of knowledge,* the *discerning of spirits.* The word of knowledge indicates an understanding of spiritual truth. The word of wisdom reveals the ability to apply spiritual truth. The discerning of spirits is the ability to know when the Spirit of God is speaking.

   There are three "worship" gifts: *prophecy, tongues, the interpretation of tongues.* Prophecy is the declaration of truth under the inspiration of the Holy Spirit. Tongues are ecstatic utterances in a pattern not previously learned by the mind. The interpretation of tongues is an accurate communication of the meaning of the ecstatic utterances.

   There are also three "power" gifts: *faith, healing, miracles.* The gift of faith refers to one's exercise of belief for accomplishment of a particular spiritual objective. A person with the gift of healing becomes the human agent in divine restoration of wholeness. The gift of miracles belongs to one who is the human agent in the divine display of a transcendent, supernatural law.

Besides the gifts, there are at least ten "administrations" of the Spirit: apostles, prophets, teachers (pastors/teachers), helps/government (administration), evangelists, ministry, exhortations, giving, ruling, showing mercy.

The nine *gifts* plus the ten *administrations* result in nineteen *operations* of the Spirit.

4. The distribution of the gifts of the Spirit is in accordance with divine wisdom. Paul writes, "All these are the work of one and the same Spirit, and he gives them to each one, just as he determines" (1 Cor. 12:11). As the offer of the gift of the Spirit is a revelation of the divine love, so the distribution of spiritual gifts is an evidence of divine sovereignty.

5. Every gift of the Spirit is to be used for the good of the total church. Gifts are not to be received as personal privileges or hoarded as spiritual treasures. "To each one the manifestation of the Spirit is given for the common good" (1 Cor. 12:7).

It is neither the privilege nor the responsibility of the Spirit-filled Christian to seek any particular gift of the Spirit for himself/herself. The Spirit is sovereign in this matter. He selects whom He will, upon whom to bestow a gift (1 Cor. 12:11). The Christian's responsibility is to be totally yielded to the Spirit and receptive to whatever He offers.

The possession of a gift of the Spirit is never the sole evidence, or even the primary evidence, of a person's having received the gift of the Spirit. But a sure evidence of the validity of a gift of the Spirit is its constructive effect upon the total body of believers. Gifts are to be used for the common good (1 Cor. 12:7), never for the dividing asunder of the body of Christ. Their use should contribute to the spiritual wholeness of the church.

Any mention of spiritual gifts calls to mind the modern

"charismatic revival." This movement is characterized by both weaknesses and strengths. For one thing, the names applied to the movement, such as "Holy Spirit revival" and "charismatic revival" are somewhat misleading. The impression is given that at last the Holy Spirit is being discovered as a spiritual novelty. Likewise, the use of the term charismatic is misleading because at the very beginning attention was focused on but one gift rather than on all the charismata. Initially it was a "glossolalia revival" because the experience of the gift of tongues was exalted as the primary identification of being Spirit-filled.

This movement has always been preoccupied with a concern for individualistic possession of the baptism of the Spirit. They have taught that what matters is for the individual to be filled with the Spirit. There has usually been an inadequate understanding of the relation of the fullness of the Spirit to the corporate body of the church. In fact, it has often been the tendency for individuals, once they claim to be filled with the Spirit, to become separatist in their attitude toward others who do not claim the same kind of spiritual experience. The movement has been characterized by certain excesses in claims about prayer, the gift of knowledge, and healing. Many have been led to believe that if a person were really Spirit-filled, every prayer would be answered in exactly the way it was made, and usually instantly. In other words, the failure to have a prayer answered means some kind of aberration in one's spiritual experience.

However, despite these weaknesses, we cannot minimize the positive effects of the charismatic revival, which has provided a fresh focus upon the person and ministry of the Holy Spirit. It has created a new concern about the gifts of the Spirit and led to a serious, intensive study of the New Testament Scriptures. Multitudes have experienced personal spiritual renewal. The movement has also sought to recall attention to ministries which in many cases have been too long neglected.

The Holy Spirit has done even more for the church across the centuries. He has preserved the Holy Scriptures, supervised their collection into an official canon known as

the Bible, and has illumined the church in its understanding
of the Scriptures. Without the Holy Spirit there would have
been no church, and without the Scriptures the life of the
church would never have been sustained. They are the basis
and guide of the faith and practice of the church. The Holy
Scriptures have been likened to a lantern, a light, a beacon, a
lamp, a casket of treasures, a banner, a chart and compass, a
heaven-drawn picture for Christ to share with all the world.
All of this is beautifully expressed in William How's poem:

> O Word of God Incarnate,
> O Wisdom from on high,
> O Truth unchanged, unchanging,
> O Light of our dark sky:
> We praise Thee for the radiance
> That from the hallowed page,
> A lantern to our footsteps,
> Shines on from age to age.

> The Church from Thee, her Master,
> Received the gift divine,
> And still that light she lifteth
> O'er all the earth to shine.
> It is the sacred casket,
> Where gems of truth are stored;
> It is the heaven-drawn picture
> Of Thee, the living Word.

> It floateth like a banner
> Before God's host unfurled;
> It shineth like a beacon
> Above the darkling world.
> It is the chart and compass
> That o'er life's surging sea,
> 'Mid mists and rocks and quicksands,
> Still guides, O Christ, to Thee.

> O make Thy Church, dear Saviour,
> A lamp of purest gold,
> To bear before the nations
> Thy true light as of old.
> O teach Thy wandering pilgrims
> By this their path to trace,

Till, clouds and darkness ended,
They see Thee face to face.

The Spirit has been the secret of the continuity of the church across the centuries, and has kept alive its spiritual effectiveness in the face of great odds. The Holy Spirit has made possible the church's victory over the threats which have struck at its very life. These have been both from without and within. During most of its existence the church has been the object of major persecution by some political power. At other times persecutions have been less widespread and more sporadic, but always a force of opposition which the church has had to survive.

Continuing threats against the life of the church have come also from within. Few periods in church history have been free from internal strife and dissension. There have been doctrinal divisions and ethical warfare. Separatism in many instances has led to ecclesiastical divisions. At times the very nature of the church has been betrayed by those who claim to be its loyal supporters—by compromises with worldliness, by pagan lifestyles, by insensitivity to spiritual values, by a lethargy in loyalty and a breakdown in commitment and support. But the church has survived; it is to be reckoned with in our world today, and all this because of the power of the Holy Spirit upon the body of Christ.

The phenomenal expansion of the Christian church across the centuries is the result of the energy of the Holy Spirit. The Spirit has been the stimulus and support of world evangelization. Even during the Dark Ages the church provided a spiritual womb for the birth of the saints; and what a heritage they have left us! They preserved the treasures of the church. We are indebted to the monasteries for the safekeeping and transmission of the Holy Scriptures. The Holy Spirit has stimulated revival, renewal, and reform across the centuries, preserving the church for future generations. The Holy Spirit has clearly been the chief actor in the dramas of the church throughout history. Let us be humbly grateful to Him.

Against this background consider now what the Holy Spirit wants to continue to do for the church.

First, the Holy Spirit wants to keep the church healthy at all times. The church is a living organism, not a sterile, static organization, unconcerned about a dynamic inner wholeness. An organism's effectiveness and growth are dependent upon its health. So the Holy Spirit wants to keep the church a functioning body. Many factors contribute to the health of the church. Basically, there is the life of the Spirit within the members and the corporate structure. Where the Spirit is in control the organism will be healthy.

One factor necessary for a healthy church, often bypassed, is a sense of unity within the church, created by the Holy Spirit. The Scriptures speak of "the unity of the Spirit" (Eph. 4:3). Paul warns Christians against schism in the body of Christ (1 Cor. 12:25). John Wesley described the church as a universal body of believers filled with and united by the Holy Spirit. The lack of unity in the church is an evidence of the absence of health, and the Holy Spirit is the secret of unity. One of the liturgies of the Orthodox Church declares, "When He distributed the tongues of fire at Pentecost, He called all men to unity, wherefore we glorify the Holy Spirit with one accord."

In Philippians 2:2 Paul states that church growth is dependent upon unity in the Spirit. Christians are to be "like-minded," "having the same love," "one in spirit and purpose." Spirit-created unity is not an intangible, uncertain thing, but on the contrary is evidence by its basis in truth and its manifestation of the bonds of love.

So unity is essential if the church is to function as God intended it. To attain unity there must be a sense of commitment on the part of each member of the church, but at the same time there must be a respectful recognition of varying areas of commitment. The common focus is Christ, and commitment to Him is the coordinating ideal that brings us all together. Neither community nor unity is created by merely exhorting Christians to achieve it. The factors that make for community must be emphasized, and when these are observed and practiced a sense of unity begins to emerge.

The Holy Spirit helps to keep the church healthy through His renewing ministry. C. S. Lewis wrote, "The entire Body of Christ needs the renewal that can come only by and in the Presence of the Holy Spirit." The Holy Spirit also wants to help the church keep its priorities focused on its redemptive mission in the entire world, to keep it on the right track. In a world characterized not only by evil institutions, but also by secular and humanistic philosophies, it is so easy for the church to lose its way. The church is primarily an agent for redemption, and this mission has never changed. It is the only distinctly spiritual institution in the world. If the church does not carry on the ministries of Christ, no other institution will. When the church starts making worldly activities a priority, two things are sure to follow. On the one hand, the church usually goes about worldly assignments in a much more haphazard, ineffective way than do secular institutions. Moreover, when the church is preoccupied with worldly pursuits, it neglects redemptive ministries, and people are denied what they should be offered in and through Christ.

Therefore, the Holy Spirit wants to help the church preserve its purity, both of doctrine, and of lifestyle. The New Testament's concern is for the church's purity. Paul exhorts Timothy to "take heed to yourself [lifestyle] and to your teaching [doctrine]" (1 Tim. 4:16, RSV). Again, Paul exhorts Titus always to show "integrity in his teaching [doctrine]" (Titus 2:7, RSV). The church at Pergamum was rebuked for becoming congenial to false doctrine—"the teaching of Balaam," "the teaching of the Nicolaitans" (Rev. 2:12–15, RSV).

But the church was also rebuked for impurity in conduct. Speaking to the church at Thyatira, Christ indicts it for "tolerating the woman Jezebel, who calls herself a prophetess and is teaching and beguiling my servants to practice immorality" (Rev. 2:20, RSV).

The ideal for the church is always that of purity. "Christ loved the church and gave himself for it, that he might sanctify the church, having cleansed the church by the washing of water with the word, that the church might be preserved before him in splendor, without spot or wrinkle or any such thing, that she might be holy and without blemish" (Eph. 5:25–27). According to the Scriptures, the heavenly life will make a clear distinction between purity and impurity: "Let the evildoer still do evil . . . and the holy still be holy" (Rev. 22:11). The pure will enter the city by the gates, but the impure will remain always on the outside (Rev. 22:14–15, RSV).

Inevitably the church is influenced by the climate of the world and of the age in which it functions. With so much wickedness prevalent everywhere, there is always the subtle tendency for the church to yield to that which surrounds it. But the Holy Spirit wants to help us to keep pure, to be in the world but not of the world, not to be conformed to the world but transformed by the power of the Spirit.

Furthermore, the Holy Spirit wants to help the church be totally relevant to the age it seeks to serve. Old Testament prophets addressed the social issues of their day (and often lost their lives because of it); Jesus in His teachings dealt with the religious and ethical problems pressing upon people during the time of His ministry; the Holy Spirit led the early church to be relevant to the problems and needs of the people it served; so in every generation the contagious, effective church has lived where the people lived, dealt with issues that were of pressing concern, and sought to make an impact upon that generation.

The Wesleyan Revival was a Spirit-inspired activity in relevance. People burdened down in the guilt and power of sin wanted to know whether deliverance and redemption were really possible. Those redeemed cried out for the experience of a holiness realizable in personal experience. The masses oppressed by unchristian social practices and inhumane laws agonized for some kind of power to enter their lives and their world to break the chains that bound them and to give them a fresh start in life. Charles Wesley summarized the spirit of relevance in the Wesleyan Revival in lines from his hymn "A Charge to Keep I Have": "To serve the present age, / My calling to fulfill."

Today's church must be fully relevant to the needs of

today. Even though the church always builds upon the proved values of tradition, it dare not live in the past. Nor dare it think only in terms of tomorrow. A musical drama has the line, "If you only pile up tomorrows you will soon discover only empty yesterdays." We must live in the present.

The church must stop answering questions that are no longer being asked. It must not spend its energies on fighting battles already won or no longer existent. The Holy Spirit wants to keep the church sensitive to contemporary human need and constantly aware of pressing issues in today's world. A new emphasis in our day insists the church must be the model and protector of spirituality in an age of dominant secular humanism. It must reproduce Christ-oriented, Spirit-filled disciples who live above the quagmire of worldliness and materialism.

A. W. Tozer has a timely word:

> The popular notion that the first obligation of the Christian Church is to spread the gospel to the uttermost parts of the earth is false!
>
> Her first obligation is to be spiritually worthy to spread the gospel.
>
> Our Lord said "Go ye" but He also said "Tarry ye," and the tarrying had to come before the going. Had the disciples gone forth as missionaries before the day of Pentecost it would have been an overwhelming spiritual disaster, for they could have done no more than make converts after their own likeness, and this would have altered for the worse the whole history of the Western world and had consequences throughout the ages to come.
>
> Theoretically the seed, being the Word of God, should produce the same kind of fruit regardless of the spiritual condition of those who scatter it; but it does not work that way! The identical message preached to the heathen by men of differing degrees of godliness will produce different kinds of converts and result in a quality of Christianity varying according to the purity and power of those who preach it.

Christianity will always reproduce after its kind. A worldly minded, unspiritual church, when she crosses the ocean to give her witness to peoples of other tongues and cultures, is sure to bring forth on other shores a Christianity much like her own!"[2]

The Holy Spirit superintends the continuity of the church and its missionary march into all nations. More than two billion persons throughout the world wait to hear the Gospel message. More than one hundred fifty million persons remain unchurched in our so-called Christian nation. The Holy Spirit wants to sound "forward march" for the church in the greatest missionary endeavor of the centuries. However, we must never lose the biblical concept of what it means to evangelize. Evangelism is more than doing good things to people. Evangelism is announcing the Good News of salvation to those outside the kingdom of Christ and inviting them to enter the kingdom.

Such continuity of the church through growth is the result of the empowerment of the Holy Spirit. Archbishop Cosmo Gordon Lang of the Church of England once declared to a church congress meeting in Southport, "It is scarcely possible to exaggerate the new strength which might come to a church which deliberately set itself to recover faith in the Holy Spirit, and to stir up the gift of Himself within it."

How tragic if the church tries to fulfill its divinely appointed mission apart from the power of the Spirit! I recall an episode in a small church in which there was prolonged bickering in relation to putting electricity in the parsonage. The usual arguments in those days were advanced by the opponents: "Other pastors did not mind the inconvenience," or "our expenses are already too heavy," etc. Finally, the church board voted to install electricity. The pastor commented, "It wasn't the inconvenience that troubled me most, but the fact that while the arguments were going on, the power line was right over the church lawn. It was available power not being used." How often the church wastes time, energy, and resources arguing about the impossibility of its task when all the time the power is waiting to be connected. We must never forget that it is not by human might or power, but always by God's Spirit.

The Holy Spirit will also guarantee continuing adequate leadership for the church, both lay and clergy. The normal mood of the church is growth. New members are to be added daily. The Spirit will also call those whom the church is to ordain. How meaningful are some lines found in one of the hymns of ordination:

> Come, Holy Ghost, our souls inspire,
> And lighten with celestial fire;
> Thou the anointing Spirit art,
> Who dost Thy sevenfold gifts impart.
> Praise to Thy eternal merit,
> Father, Son and Holy Spirit.

The Spirit also provides a ministry of the laity. Each person is enabled to find an area of service. Each person is to be developed so that he will be all that God wants him to be. In the New Testament sense, every Christian is a minister. In Ephesians 4:12 Paul declares that spiritual gifts were given "to prepare God's people for works of service."

Jean Hamilton wrote an interesting article entitled, "All of My Friends Are Ministers . . . and Some of Them Are Ordained." She said that (1) lay ministry is as full time as ordained ministry; (2) the lay minister must be as committed to Christ as the ordained minister; (3) the lay minister can perform ministries that the ordained minister cannot, and vice versa; (4) it is unfortunate to speak of ordained ministry as a "higher" calling.[3]

The Holy Spirit will also provide for adequate financial support of the church by dedicated persons whom the Spirit inspires to be faithful stewards. When a church proposes to be a vital part of the body of Christ and yet there are devastating financial problems, something is wrong somewhere. It certainly isn't that God is not able to provide. The Spirit-filled church is the adequate church financially.

Finally, the Holy Spirit wants to continue to inspire the church with the hope of its eternal triumph. Jesus said, "On this rock I will build my church, and the gates of Hades will not overcome it" (Matt. 16:18). The apostle John was permitted to glimpse the outcome of it all: "The kingdoms of this world are becoming the *kingdoms* of our Lord, and of his Christ; and he shall reign for ever and ever" (Rev. 11:15, KJV). Colin Morris said, "When computers are employed to make predictions, we would be foolish and faithless to ignore in our calculations factor X known as the Holy Spirit."

> O where are kings and empires now,
> Of old that went and came?
> But, Lord, Thy Church is praying yet,
> A thousand years the same.
>
> We mark her goodly battlements
> And her foundations strong;
> We hear within the solemn voice
> Of her unending song.
>
> For not like kingdoms of the world
> Thy holy Church, O God!
> Tho' earthquake shocks are threatening her,
> And tempests are abroad;
>
> Unshaken as eternal hills,
> Immovable she stands,
> A mountain that shall fill the earth,
> A house not made with hands.
>
> (A. Cleveland Coxe)

Never forget that the Holy Spirit is at work *now* in the contemporary church in distinctive and significant ways. My friend Kenneth Kinghorn published a book entitled *Fresh Winds of the Spirit.*[4] How expressive this title is! Columnist Louis Cassells once wrote, "Something new and infinitely hopeful is taking place. It is a rediscovery of the dynamic reality which the early Christian community called 'the power of the Spirit' . . . Emphasis on the power of the Spirit is undergoing a remarkable resurgence across the entire spectrum of Christian denominations."

This new focus upon the person and work of the Holy

Spirit affects particularly the mainline denominations. Lay persons are asking questions about the Holy Spirit. Clergy are engaged in specialized studies. Local churches abound with study groups focused on the Holy Spirit. Conferences on the Holy Spirit are held frequently.

One such conference of international significance was held at Oslo, Norway, in 1985. It brought together participants from thirty nations, from the full spectrum of the global evangelical constituency. The gathering, which had been regarded as a theological function, took on the complexion of a revival meeting when nearly two hours were devoted to prayers of confession, worship, and pleas for personal cleansing. Participants sought to establish a consensus on the person and work of the Holy Spirit. They discussed fundamental perspectives and more controversial themes, such as the gifts of the Spirit, including healing, speaking in tongues, and exorcism.

The consultation's final statement called for equal emphasis on holiness and power. That balanced emphasis, declared participants, is the crux of the Holy Spirit's role in world evangelization. The gifts of the Spirit and the fruit of the Spirit are equally important. Neglect of one, or preoccupation with either, stunts the church and represents an inadequate understanding of the Gospel.

Here are a few representative statements from the Oslo Declaration:

> World evangelization is the central task of the Church. The Holy Spirit was poured out on the day of Pentecost to equip God's people for this global task.
>
> The Holy Spirit is the missionary spirit. He, therefore, urges the whole church to bring the whole gospel to the whole world.
>
> The gift of the Holy Spirit was poured out at Pentecost on the whole Church and not on isolated individuals. The Spirit gives his gifts as he wills to individual members in order to build up the body of Christ for evangelism and service to the world.

Renewal by the Spirit brings new life to existing church structures and may create new structures to serve the gospel.

Sanctification is the work of the Holy Spirit, dwelling in God's people both individually and corporately in an ongoing process of holiness.

We believe that the Church filled with the Holy Spirit will respond faithfully, joyfully, and eagerly to the evangelization of the yet unreached peoples of the world.

In this time of renewal, the significance of the local church is seen in a new light, and there is a growing reaction against excessive institutionalism and ecclesiasticism. Many areas see significant growth in membership, attendance, and giving, together with a deepening concern for evangelism.

Innumerable renewal movements within major denominational bodies encourage concern for evangelicalism in theological education. And evangelicals are increasingly taking the initiative to apply the gospel to social situations and issues. Carl F. H. Henry, the dean of American evangelicals, has pleaded, "The time is long overdue for evangelical witness and involvement in the social crisis in America." Evangelicals are increasingly prominent in social leadership. And can it not be said confidently that evangelical involvement in social issues has given a stability and effectiveness to social action because of sound biblical and theological undergirding? Evangelicals begin with loving God—then move out to love others. To try to love and serve others without a devotion and commitment to Jesus Christ first of all, sooner or later wears thin and leads to disillusionment.

Another evidence of the Spirit's activity in the church today is the amazing manifestation of the autonomy of churches in the developing countries of the world, which were formerly considered mission churches. In spite of opposition and setbacks, the past few decades have witnessed phenomenal developments in what we know as Christian missions. Take the United Methodist Church as just one illustration. Less than half a century ago most of the

Methodist churches outside the United States were superintended either by bishops elected in the United States or by missionaries from this country. Now, almost without exception, those churches have become autonomous and function under the leadership of national Christians elected by their peers.

One impressive activity of the Spirit today is the amazing resurgence of Christian churches behind the various "curtains" erected by governments hostile to Christianity. We do not have the full story of the church behind the Iron Curtain or the Bamboo Curtain, but every report emanating from these areas gives indications that, far from being eradicated during days of government opposition, the church maintained astonishing vitality. Now with the lessening of some restrictions, it is manifesting great growth and activity.

Reports from China offer a thrilling illustration. In spite of relentless efforts of the Cultural Revolution to stamp out every vestige of faith in God, the underground church multiplied vigorously. Bibles are in short supply and training is difficult to obtain, but house churches number in the hundreds of thousands, and more people appear to be turning to Christ than ever before. Large numbers have even undertaken intensive evangelistic journeys to distant places. One reliable source reports that house churches are known to exist in almost all of China's 2,007 counties. G. D. James, founder of Asia Evangelistic Fellowship, has stated:

> The church in China is small compared to the vast exploding population. But it is stronger than when it was largely under Western leadership. The fires of persecutions and problems . . . have purified the church . . . and produced dynamic and responsible leadership among national missions and missionaries. All this has given the Asian church credibility, identity, and dignity unknown thirty years ago.

All these are evidences of the contemporary activity of the Holy Spirit in the church. But it should be noted that there are dramatic evidences of the Spirit's activity in the secular world as well. First, there is an amazing spirit of creativity evident in the world of knowledge, research, and discovery. Is not the Holy Spirit at work even in modern technology, with His added stimulus that such progress be dedicated to the welfare of persons and the betterment of the world? A growing respect for God's creation, for the care of natural resources, is also a sign of the breathing of the Spirit.

Finally, evident in so many ways is the yearning of secular humankind for some kind of satisfying theological support for one's being. This expresses itself in modern literature, art, and music, and in the expressed inner longing of philosophers, historians, scientists, and enlightened politicians.

In summary, it seems appropriate to conclude that generally speaking, what the Holy Spirit wants to do for the church is to make it and keep it and use it as "the church of the Spirit." This phrase was proposed by Francis G. Peabody. He draws a clear and decisive line between what he terms "the church of authority" and "the church of the Spirit." Those who are primarily concerned with a dogmatic expression of Christianity in an institution adhere to the church of authority. It is a visible church, characterized by stability, continuity, and legality. It proposes the way of conformity as the test of Christian loyalty and insists upon the acceptance of the Christian religion as a governmental scheme.

In contrast to the church of authority, another type of faith and fellowship, which may be spoken of as the church of the Spirit, has coexisted with it through all the years of Christian history. The church of the Spirit offers a form of discipleship less easily defined because it is progressive, expanding, and spiritual. To the church of the Spirit, the most precious incidents of Christian history may not be those of theological or ecclesiastical transition, but those of religious revival—the testimony of saints and seers, the experience of holy souls, the convincing evidence of the life of God in the souls of persons.

The church of the Spirit has been described as an inflowing, refreshing, penetrating tide. The church of the

Spirit, in subordinating opinions to obedience and dogmatics to loyalty, makes the audacious assertion that often the church of authority, in its institutional procedure, has been tempted to take the wrong road, making central what was incidental, setting logic before life, speculation before inspiration, the letter before the Spirit.

Peabody contrasts the two in these significant words:

> Here, then are two ways of Christian loyalty—the way of conformity and the way of consecration; the acceptance of the Christian religion as a governmental scheme, and the recognition of the Christian religion as a spiritual experience. . . . The fundamental difference is not so much in the desire for discipleship as in the way of approach to discipleship. One way is through intellectual consent; the other is though volitional consecration. To the one the chief agent of faith is the mind; to the other it is the will. The one teaching begins: He that knoweth the doctrine shall do the will; the other begins: Whosoever willeth to do the will shall know of the doctrine.[5]

Peabody remarks that whereas the greatest internal danger to a church of authority is that of nonconformity, the sins of a church of the Spirit are to be found in spiritual defections and moral delinquencies. He mentions four sins peculiar to the church of the Spirit: spiritual illiteracy, spiritual complacency, spiritual indolence, spiritual intolerance.

In our desire for the church of the Spirit, we must become aware of the presence of any of these spiritual conditions in the church and see that they are dealt with satisfactorily.

Spiritual illiteracy does not refer primarily to a kind of academic ignorance. Rather, it refers to a lack of sensitivity to spiritual influences. The remedy is the baptism and control of the Holy Spirit. The Spirit transforms us into an awareness of spiritual reality through His renewing of our minds.

The sin of spiritual complacency refers to the church's inactivity because of self-satisfaction. The church becomes satisfied with what it has already done. There is no creative thrust for fresh activity in the present or future. The antidote to spiritual complacency is to be found in a valid use of the gifts of the Spirit. Certainly through the bestowal of any of His gifts the Spirit calls the believer to renewed and creative activity in the name of Jesus Christ.

Spiritual indolence refers to mistaken notions about the manner in which grace operates in the Christian's life. Some believe that once divine grace is received by an individual, all of the consequences and potential of such grace become automatic in a person's life. How far from the truth! One must respond continuously to appropriated grace and cooperate with it increasingly. Paul reminds us that because God works in us we must work out our own salvation with fear and trembling (Phil. 2:12–13).

Just so in the life of the church. Even though the power of the Holy Spirit is available at all times, it must be appropriated and utilized. There must be an increasing sensitivity to the Spirit's presence, and channels must be kept open for the power of the Holy Spirit to flow.

Another sin of the church of the Spirit is spiritual intolerance. This has been described as "the sin of small minds in their dealings with great themes." How eruptive is the tendency for our small minds, in dealing with such great themes as spiritual experience, the church, and the Christian mission to make us narrow in our attitudes and in our conduct.

Frank Laubach once commented:

> We all tend to shut ourselves out from God's myriad channels because we insist on God flowing down through our particular denominational or social or political channel. The dryness of many a saint has resulted from his closing off every pipe line except one. It is dreadful how sectarianism makes men consider goodness sinful unless it flows down their own ecclesiastical ditch.[5]

When such sectarianism becomes intolerance the church needs to be reminded of the unity which the Spirit creates.

The antidote to the sin of spiritual intolerance is found in the Great Commission. The Spirit calls us to world evangelization. "The Spirit and the bride say, 'Come!' And let him who hears say, 'Come!' Whoever is thirsty, let him come; and whoever wishes, let him take the free gift of the water of life" (Rev. 22:17). Will not the faithful stewardship of the Spirit's commission inevitably create a bond of spiritual unity? Is not the evangelization of the world too mighty a task to try to do alone?

"The church of the Spirit"—what a heritage!—what a privilege!—what a stewardship! Ours is the responsibility to manifest in contemporary life the genius of the church of the Spirit in His ever available presence and power.

EPILOGUE

I BELIEVE IN THE HOLY SPIRIT

I believe in God the Father . . . I believe in Jesus Christ
. . . I believe in the Holy Spirit. . . ."

The Apostles' Creed

Throughout the Christian centuries the oldest creed of
the church has exhorted Christians to believe in the Holy
Spirit. Unfortunately, during much of the time, the church
has acted as if it underbelieved in the Holy Spirit. In more
recent decades, in the midst of some of the excesses of the
so-called Holy Spirit renewal movement, some Christians
have seemed to overbelieve in Him. But the Scriptures, the
traditions of the church, and personal spiritual experience all
call upon us to believe in the Holy Spirit. In the final
analysis, what we believe is the all-important issue.

THE HOLY SPIRIT IS ALWAYS AT WORK, EVERYWHERE

The Holy Spirit is God and Christ at work in the world.
This activity is both the evidence of the continuing creativity
of God and the present authenticity of the resurrection of
Jesus Christ. The Holy Spirit does not have to be coaxed to
work; He has only to be given an opportunity. We give Him
opportunity by removing all hindrances.

He works both in predictable and unpredictable ways.
For instance, the Bible predicts that He will be enlightening

117

and convicting and inspiring. When we perform any of the spiritual ministries characteristic of New Testament Christianity, we can be confident that the Holy Spirit has already promised to work through them.

But we must always make room for the unpredictable activities of the Holy Spirit. This is a universe not only of the predictable, but also of the unpredictable. Scientists often write about our surprising universe, how suddenly something will appear or something will happen in the physical universe that nobody expected. The Spirit also works this way. Jesus, likening the Spirit to the wind, said that "it blows where it wills." We see it in divine providence. We see it in answers to prayer. We see it in divine guidance. We see it in revival movements. We see it in miracles of healing. We see it in certain social revolutions.

This implies that the Spirit is continually speaking to the church. An exhortation in the book of the Revelation occurs as a continuing refrain after each of the seven churches is addressed: "Hear what the Spirit says to the churches" (Rev. 2:7, 11, 17, 29; 3:6, 13, 22).

The Holy Spirit has talked to the church in every age. He talked to the Old Testament "church" about ethical righteousness, the coming of the Messiah and His kingdom, the inauguration of a New Covenant. He talked to the New Testament church, dramatically on the first day of Pentecost and persistently to remind the church of the teachings of Jesus. The Spirit's dealings with each of the seven churches in Revelation is symbolic of the Spirit's relationship to all churches in all centuries. The particular spiritual focus of the church in each period of history and the unfolding trends in the church's life and activity in succeeding centuries are evidence of the inspiration of the Holy Spirit.

Just so, the Spirit is speaking to the church today. But we must have ears to hear. A worldly church is not alert to the Spirit's voice. There must be spiritual responsiveness. Listen! The Spirit is speaking. Do you hear what He is saying? He is reminding the church that His presence and power are available at all times, that when we have even the least tendency to stray, the Spirit calls us back to our redemptive priorities.

The Spirit tells the church never to forget its past. He is not suggesting any discontinuity in spiritual history nor any innovation in divine revelation. The church is "built upon the foundation of the apostles and prophets, Christ Jesus Himself being the chief cornerstone, in whom the whole structure is joined together and grows into a holy temple in the Lord; in whom you also are built into it for a dwelling place of God in the Spirit" (Eph. 2:20–22, RSV). Every evangelical witness is based upon tradition as the undergirding of experience. So the Holy Spirit encourages us to appreciate the continuity in theology, in worship and hymnody, and in mission across the centuries.

The church stands constantly in need of renewal. Elton Trueblood wrote:

> I find that I must employ at least four adjectives to describe the faith by which I now try to live. Consequently, when I am asked what I am, spiritually, I sometimes reply that I am a "catholic," "apostolic," "reformed," "evangelical" Christian. . . .
>
> I try to be "catholic" in the sense that I want to be universal in my faith, not leaving aside any truths merely because they do not happen to be part of my own tradition. The primary opposite to catholic is sectarian. . . .
>
> The reason why our faith must be apostolic is that we need a firm point of reference. . . . We need the apostolic emphasis because it is not sufficient to be contemporary. We need roots, and the apostolic faith provides such roots in abundance. . . .
>
> The word "reformed" which is often a synonym for "Protestant" is an excellent one. There are many spiritual dangers "in protesting," but these do not appear in "reforming." The true reformer is always working for renewal, and he is humble enough to realize that, so far as each individual is concerned, it must begin with himself. . . .

The fourth feature of an adequate faith . . . is that it be evangelical, in the precise sense that it is Christ—centered. . . . My own basic faith is increasingly Christ-centered, because in Christ, I find something undeniably stable and definite. . . ."[1]

The Spirit has not yet completed the process of building the church. It is still under construction. We are in danger of criticizing the church because we do not like its incompleteness. Rather should we "stick in there," cooperating fully with the Spirit in helping Him build the church.

Certainly the Spirit talks about His exclusive use of spiritual means and spiritual forces in carrying on His ministry, and He establishes faith as the normal climate of the people of God. He inspires the church to declare to the world that it is not by earthly might but by the living Spirit of God that things that really matter are accomplished. The amazing strength of contemporary power—scientific, technological, industrial, institutional—must never be allowed to depreciate the transcendence of spiritual power. It is the Holy Spirit who is the dynamite of God.

The Holy Spirit is the divine agent in redemption at every stage of spiritual experience. This is illustrated in the Wesleyan "order of salvation." Wesleyans believe in prevenient grace, the sense of conviction for sin, the actualities of repentance and faith, the experience of initial salvation in justification and regeneration, and the witness of the Spirit. The Holy Spirit is the active agent to effect all these experiences.

I affirm life-in-the-Spirit as well as belief-in-the-Spirit and experience-in-the-Spirit. Sanctification has been described as a flower of three petals: a doctrine to be believed; an experience to be received; a life to be achieved.

The ministry of the Holy Spirit is indissolubly related to Jesus Christ and His church. When we are filled with the Holy Spirit, we do not bypass either Christ or the church. The Holy Spirit never betrays Jesus Christ nor does the Spirit ever seek to depreciate the church before the world. If one's experience is leading him around either Christ or the church, he is not following the Holy Spirit.

The Holy Spirit wants to work through each of us to bless others. Each of us can have all of the Holy Spirit's power and ministrations whenever needed, if we only learn and observe the spiritual law of demand and supply. Frank Laubach summarized this truth well: "The water of life will flow to us only if it flows through us."[2]

The Holy Spirit is the Spirit of hope. The mood of the early church, in the words of John Henry Jowett, was that of apostolic optimism. It is the Spirit who seeks always to inspire such a spiritual climate. The Spirit gives us the hope that we will be victorious as Christians. We shall overcome! He gives the hope that the ministries of the church will be effective. The best days of the church must be ahead. The Holy Spirit inspires us with the confidence that Christ is *in* history, that God is working out His purposes now in our world, and that ultimately the kingdom of this world will become the kingdom of our Lord and of His Christ; and Christ will reign forever and ever (Rev. 11:15). Hallelujah!

NOTES

CHAPTER 1

[1] Samuel H. Moffatt, "Where's the Power?" *Princeton Seminary Bulletin* 6, no. 2 (1985): 59–67.

[2] R. Newton Flew, *The Idea of Perfection in Christian Theology* (London: Oxford University Press, 1934).

[3] E. Stanley Jones, *How to Be a Transformed Person* (New York: Abingdon-Cokesbury, 1951), 141–47.

CHAPTER 2

[1] E. Stanley Jones, *Mastery: The Art of Mastering Life* (Nashville: Abingdon, 1955), 23.

CHAPTER 3

[1] Richard H. Popkin, "Blaise Pascal," *Encyclopedia of Philosophy*, 6:52.

[2] James C. Fenhagen, *Ministry and Solitude: The Ministry of the Laity and Clergy in Church and Society* (New York: Seabury, 1981), 133.

[3] David L. Thompson, "Kuhn, Kohlberg and Kinlaw: Reflections for Over-serious Theologians," *Wesleyan Theological Journal* 19, no. 1 (Spring 1984), 17.

[4] Noel Coward, *Hay Fever* (New York: Harper & Brothers, 1925), Act II.

[5] Thomas Merton, *The Sign of Jonas* (London: Hollis and Carter, 1953).

[6] Oswald Chambers, *My Utmost for His Highest* (New York: Dodd, Mead, 1935), 106.

[7] Al Bryant, *The John Wesley Reader* (Waco, Tex.: Word, 1983), 261–70.

[8] Gerald Heard, *Prayers and Meditations* (New York: Harper, 1949), 58.

[9] Amy Carmichael, *Whispers of His Power* (Old Tappan, N. J.: Revell, 1982), 8–9.

[10] Chambers, *Utmost*, 337.

[11] Corrie ten Boom, *Tramp for the Lord* (Fort Washington, Pa.: Christian Literature Crusade, 1974), 57.

[12] Thomas Kepler, *An Anthology of Devotional Literature* (New York: Abingdon-Cokesbury, 1948), 8.

CHAPTER 4

[1] Thomas C. Upham, *Inward Divine Guidance* (Syracuse, N.Y.: Wesleyan Methodist Publishing Association, 1905).

[2] Paul Tournier, *The Seasons of Life* (Richmond: John Knox, 1963), 44.

[3] Thomas Merton, *Thoughts in Solitude* (New York: Farrar, Straus and Cudahy, 1958), 83.

[4] William Barclay, *The Mind of Jesus* (New York: Harper, 1961), 67.

CHAPTER 5

[1] F. W. Dillistone, *The Holy in the Life of Today* (Philadelphia: Westminster, 1957), 34–35.

[2] A. W. Tozer, *Renewed Day by Day,* ed. G. B. Smith (Harrisburg, Pa.: Christian Publications, 1980), December 14.

[3] Jean Hamilton, "All of My Friends Are Ministers . . . and Some of Them Are Ordained," *United Church Observer* 39 (March 1976): 26–28.

[4] Kenneth Cain Kinghorn, *Fresh Wind of the Spirit* (Grand Rapids: Zondervan/Francis Asbury Press, 1975).

[5] Francis G. Peabody, *The Church of the Spirit* (New York: MacMillan, 1925), 37, 39.

[6] Frank Laubach, *Channels of Spiritual Power* (Westwood, N. J.: Revell, 1954), 73–74.

EPILOGUE

[1] Elton Trueblood, *Quarterly Yoke Letter* vol. XXVII, no. 3 (September 1985).

[2] Laubach, *Channels* (Westwood, N.J.: Revell, 1954), 71, 72, 78.

LINCOLN CHRISTIAN COLLEGE AND SEMINARY